365

Joyful Poems

Lon Wartman

"365 Joyful Poems," by Lon Wartman. ISBN 978-1-63868-014-7 (softcover); 978-1-63868-015-4 (eBook).

Published 2021 by Virtualbookworm.com Publishing Company. P.O. Box 9949, College Station, TX 77842. Copyright 2021 by Lon Wartman. All rights reserved. No part of this publication may be reproduced, stored in a retrieval system, or transmitted in any form or by any means, electronic, mechanical, recording or otherwise, without the prior permission of Lon Wartman.

Introduction

This book came about as my way of coping with the COVID-19 pandemic. I decided that I wanted to write a story book of 365 joyful poems in 365 days, or less. Thus, its title "365 Joyful Poems". I began this journey on June 22, 2020, and much to my surprise completed the 365 poems on March 2, 2021. The primary purpose of this journey was to bring a little bit of joy to myself as well as those who may read it.

The pandemic along with a variety of social injustices has caused tremendous resentment, and depression to a vast number of people in our country. So much so that we need more "feel good" poetry. It is my opinion that we cannot exist in a constant state of isolation, division and hate for long periods of time. We need to cure ourselves of these bad habits. One way to do this is to train ourselves to think and write happy and joyful thoughts while at the same time recognizing and supporting the need for a more just and honorable society. Needless to say, this past year has seen a lot of tragedies; unforeseen when I began this journey. Hopefully, my words will help you cope with these depressing times. It is time for us to look for the joy in our lives rather than the sad.

The poems that I have written do not tell a story per say but are an anthology of what was going on in my brain at the time they were penned. I set several standards for these poems,
1) That they should not convey negative thoughts.
2) That they should not use negative words.
3) That they give each and every one of us hope and an inward feeling of happiness.
4) No depressing poems allowed.
5) That even if they don't make any sense, they shower a little joy in your daily lives.

I begin with a few poems describing the task at hand which is to build a bridge over a river. The valley through which the river flows is named "Despair". The bridge is to be name "JOY". The poems are intended to be the building blocks that complete this task. Hopefully when the 365 poems have been written this awful period in our lives will no longer be with us and we are back to leading normal and enjoyable lives. I realize first and foremost that some of the poems will not move the rector scale to any degree and some are just really bad. However, I hope some blow the boots off your socks and make you laugh. I also have to admit that due to some of the tragic events that happened during the past year I did lose my trail as emotions overcame my desire to write only happy poems. For that I apologize. As tragic as this time has been we all must understand that there will be emotional consequences far beyond what the eye can see.

Cover Photograph (Image Credit)

The cover photograph is titled "Ho'oK". It is a painting by the famous artist, Ted DeGrazia. This painting hangs in the "DeGrazia Gallery in the Sun" in Tucson Arizona. Ho'oK was a wicked witch with the talons of an eagle and a large appetite for children. To stop the witch from eating their children, the Papagos summoned Eetoi to help them. Eetoi drank and danced with the witch until she fell asleep. Eetoi carried the witch to her cave where he sealed her in and lit her on fire. When the witch tried to escape, Eetoi put his huge foot on a boulder at the mouth of the cave and kept Ho'oK inside until the witch died.

I found the painting to be very reflective of the days of our lives that have been stolen from us and in our battle to overcome the depression that has come with this pandemic. Indeed, it was a daily battle and the writing of the poems was my way of coming to terms with it. I choose "Joy" over depression. It was my way of putting my foot on a boulder at the mouth of the COVID cave

An original copy of this painting was provided by the Gallery and is used with the permission of the Gallery.

Dedication

I dedicate this book to my wonderful wife, Donna, who has had the fortitude to put up with me on this very trying and at times difficult journey.

"Reformation"

I wrote a poem
A long time ago
It was full of despair
And gray cloudy skies
It made me cry

I then saw a child
Playing in a park
Laughing and full of joy
I wrote no more
Of gray cloudy skies

Contents

Waste not	16
Rise up	17
Praise	18
Smiling Faces	19
Wonderful Ways	20
Gifts	21
Mr. Bo Jangles & I	22
Help	23
Sunflowers	24
Sail Away	25
Here Comes the Sun	26
Pump it Up	28
Imaginations	29
Alluring	30
Laying Stones	31
Independence Day	32
Flowers	33
Prayer	35
Happy Days	36
Happy Days-2	37
Simple Things	37
Shared Moments	38
Taking Advantage	38
Sacrifice	38
Stupid Confusion	40
There Comes A Time	41
Have you Forgotten	42
Have you Forgotten-2	43
Sunflowers	44
Caring	45
Sprinkling Sunshine	46
Sprinkling Sunshine on Your Flowers	47
Sharing Stars	48
Discovering Beauty	50
Trust	51
Sometimes	52
Anticipation	53
Balloons	55
Rocky Roads	56

Photo 1

Waterfall	57	Photo-2
Joys	58	
Amazing	59	
Snaps and Snips	60	
Reminisce	61	
Trails	62	
Trials	63	
The Farmer Said	64	
Little Squirrel	64	
Silly Day	65	
Dancing in the Street	66	
Searching	68	
Sparkles	69	
So Proud	70	
Convictions	71	
Alluring-2	72	
Good Ol Boys & Their Toys	73	
Coffee Cup Café	74	
Word Of The Day	76	
Pillars of Peace	77	
Ode To A Beauty	79	
Rewind	80	
Sashay	82	
Wonders	83	
Running	84	
A Day In The Park	86	
My Palm Tree	87	Photo 3
Why	88	
I Drew A Blank	89	
Lost But Not Lost	89	
Topless	92	
Leave Us With A Smile	93	
Calling All	94	
Turn The Music Up	96	
Set The Stage	97	
Let's Take A Walk	98	
The Gardener	99	
Here's To	100	
My New Name	101	
Word of the Day	102	
I Don't Know	103	
It Took All Day	105	
Spilling Red Wine	106	

Pesky Little Pest	106
Aphrodisiac	108
Saying Good By	109
Flowers For My Love	110
Spice For My Soul	111
Let It Rain	112
You Made My Day	113
You Never Know	114
Wonderment	115
Fantastic Words	116
Practice Perfects	117
Liquid Diets	118
Can I Borrow A Smile	118
Screw It	119
The Little Things	119
Landscapes	121 Photo 4
Pheromones	122
Scented Words	123
Smilestones	124
A Journey Is A Journey	125
Yeas & Nays	126
Spare Me	126
My Notebook	127
The End	128
Mysterious	129
Feel the Words	130
Giving Life	132
They Are	133
They Are Choices	134
Love Songs	135
Beaming	136
49 Years	138
Done In	139
Sharing	139
Caring	140
The Power of Color	144
Color it Purple	145
Color it Black	146
Color it Pink	147
Color it Green	148
Color it Blue	150
Color it Yellow	151
Color it Brown	152

Color it White	153
Color it Orange	154
Color it Red	155
Treasures	157
Donna My Love	159
Surprises	160
Surprises-2	161
Crossing Over	162
Rhythms	164
Your Smiling Face	165
Haikus "Nature's Moments"	166
Two Trails	166
A Boot in the Ass	167
Equine Rhythms	168
Adventure	169
What the Hell	170
Kiss Me	171
Last of the Haikus	172
Gladly Meets Happy	173
Free	175
Free to Be	175
Mind and Body	176
The Price You Pay	177
Rhythm of Words	178
Choose Not	179
Unusual Words	181
Mix it Up	182
Call it Home	183
Short Song-etts	184
Nothing But Bliss	185
Color Me	185
Moon Glow	185
Cat Tales	186
Notebooks-2	187
This is My Day	187
Redecorate	188
Collections	189
Wine Tales	190
Lonely	190
Confused	190
Forgetful	191
Blew That One	191
The Prize	191

How to Lose Your Lover	192	
Share Your Happy	192	
Home	193	
Home Is	195	
Waves	197	
Let's Go Charming	198	
Incredible	200	
Happy Birthday Florence	201	
Encouragement	203	
Tulips	204	Photo 5
Joy Spirits	205	
Hey! Hey!	206	
Tidbits	207	
Tidbits-2	207	
Tidbits-3	208	
The Little Things-2	208	
Will I Be Me	209	
Rise Up	210	
Bucket of Joys	211	
Heigh Ho	212	
In Search of Dopamine	214	
A Village Without A Name	215	
Rock Star	217	
Up High	218	
Caring	220	
Tricks	220	
Violent Storm	221	
Enjoyments	222	
The Gardener-2	222	
Mountain Climber	223	
The Reader	223	
Dancers	224	
Players	225	
The Fisherman	227	
The Singers	228	
Just Sing	229	
The Poet	229	
Finding Joys	230	
Joys	231	
Seeing Joy	231	
Every Night I Pray	233	
Dreaming	234	
Live Joyfully	235	

Little Barefoot Boy	236	
Little Barefoot Girl	237	
Daydream Boys	238	
Fishing	239	
Writing Love Songs	240	
Little Words	241	
Moments	241	
Brain Waves	242	
Ain't Got No Blues	243	
Serenity	244	
Find A New Joy	245	
Life's Melodrama	246	
Sexy Letters	247	
S Is Sexy Too	247	
The Letter T	248	
Other Love Letters	248	
A Sheet of Paper	249	
Girders of Love	250	
Moving On	251	
Brave Men	252	
Sweet Dreams	253	
Priming The Brain	254	
No Matter What The Scene	255	Photo 6
They Laughed	256	
Gems	257	
Halloween Night	259	
Changing the Guard	261	
Toasts	262	
For You Ladies	263	
Roses And Rainbows	263	
Bird Man	264	
Rhapsody In Democracy	266	
Tidbits-4	267	
Tidbits-5	267	
Tidbits-6	267	
Tidbits-7	267	
Onward We March	268	
Digging For Nuts	269	
This Old Car	270	
Beautiful Lines	271	
Simplicity	272	
Ballad of Billy Joe Bob	273	
Beer Belly Bob's	274	

The Joy Man	277	
Never Lost	279	
A Change is Coming	281	
Frost Fairies	282	
First Snow	285	
A Winter's Day	287	
A Wreath of Life	288	
From the Heart	289	
Borrowed Paintings	290	Photo 7
Laying Planks	291	
My Undraped Lover	292	
Halos	293	
Creative Possibilities	294	
Kindness	295	
An Affair	296	
Don't Be a Fool	297	
Enchanted Forest	298	Photo 8
Inspiration	301	
Simple Pleasures	302	
Sit, Sat & Set	303	
Sit, Sat & Set-2	303	
Situations	304	
No Regrets	305	
Things	306	
Curiosity	307	
Wanderings	308	
The Poet's Fare	309	
Transcendence	310	
Summer's Past	311	Photo 9
Prescriptions	312	
The Prairie	315	
Desert Morning	317	Photo 10
Smiles	318	
Reformation-2	319	
A Mountain Melody	319	
Reformation-3	321	Photo 11
Times Square @ Three AM	322	Photo 12
Times Square @ Three AM, Dancers	323	Photo 13
This Hallowed Eve	324	
Christmas Eve Cowgirl	325	
Old Cowboys and Cowgirls	325	
Reality Checks	326	
Manhood	327	

Reality Checks-II	328	
Jerry Lee	328	
Very Bad Santa Crawl	329	Photo 14
Good Riddance	331	
A Poetic Love Affair	332	
Voyage	333	
Caged	333	
I Am A Simple Man	334	
Smilestone-300	335	
Beauty	336	
December Glow	337	
Lost Dreams	337	
Change The Script	338	
So Proud	339	
Hey Days	339	
Good Riddance To 2020	341	
Decisions	342	
Sunshine	343	
That Song	343	
Help	344	
Decoding	344	
Ode to Old Dink	346	
A Simple Kiss	348	
Rainbows	349	
Journeys	350	
Lightning	350	
Second Thoughts	351	
Opportune	351	
Flower Garden	351	
Inspired	352	
Satisfaction	352	
Awesome	352	
Gratitude	353	
Happiness	353	
I Am Your Constitution	354	
Together We stand	357	
Hope Crystals	357	Photo on 15
Rendezvous	362	
Running Wild	363	
Revolution	364	
It's Infectious	365	
Vagrant Thoughts	366	
Cosmic Relationships	367	

Sequel to Cosmic Relationships	367
Cosmos	368
Now	368
A Poets Verse	369
Rise Up	369
Questions	370
Moments	370
Simple Pleasures	371
It Is What It Is	372
Selfies	372
Little Boys	373
The Eternal Optimist	373
Changing Courses	374
To My Sweet Valentine	374
I Am Who I Am	375
Fifteen Planks	376
Winter's Wrath	377
Worlds Apart	379	Photo 16
Why I Write Joy	381
Sail Away	382
Afternoon Delight	383
Lovers	383
Snow Flurries	383
Oh, To Be A Poem	384
I Would Love To Be That Poem	385
I Would Love To Be The Poem	385
I Would Love To Be The Poem # 2	385
I Would Love To Be The Poem # 3	386
I Would Love To Be The Poem # 4	386
I Would Love To Be The Poem # 5	386
I Would Love To Be The Poem # 365	387
The End of My Journey	388

Day-1 "Waste Not"

We have
A hill to climb
A sky to fly
An ocean to swim

So many things
So little time
Let us not waste
Our moment of sun

Sing a song of love
That knows no color
Write a verse
Without a curse

For those you
Do not know,
Praise anyway

Paint a city
As a blind man would
Speak to others
As though they were angels

Dance to a song that has no end.
Turn cartwheels in the sand
Ride cable cars to the moon
Say "Hello" to all who pass

Find joy in all you do.
Let us not waste
Our moment of sun

6/22/2020 #1

Day-2 "Rise Up"

Rise up my friends
Rise up!
Lend me a hand
We have a bridge to build

Wash the sleep from your eyes
Gather your tools
Lace up your boots
We have a bridge to build

The sun is rising
Over the distant vale
Beckoning us to sing
A song of praise
To all it has to bring

We have a bridge to build
Over the "Valley of Despair"
It will span 365 leagues
Its name plate will read

    "JOY"

Rise up my friends
Rise up
We have a bridge to build

                            6/23/2020 #2

Day-3 "Praise"

Out of the mist and fog
Of a dewdrop morn
A ghostly word came calling
A word rarely spoken
Carried on the backs
Of pied pipers two

A word that sparkles
With majestic meanings
A word that shines
Even in the black of blackest nights

Giver of life
To young and old
To friend and foe
Raises mountains from the plains
Builds lives that do not bend
Gives purpose to the striven

Empties the soul
Of wayward thoughts
Graces the feast
Laid at our feet

A word rarely spoken
A word often in need
No matter where
No matter when

A word most
Cannot live without

      "Praise"

Give it a try
Sing it out loud   6/24/2020 #3

Day-4 "Smiling Faces"

There is no place
Like a smiling face
It sets the pace
It makes the case
For a happy heart

It's a cinnamon tart
All spicy and smart

No frowns allowed
Said the sign on the door
Tis not a place for disgruntled souls
All we sell is happy inside

There is nothing to hide
Your face much prettier
When graced with a smile
Your life more buoyant
Times more enjoyed

Yours to unstitch
Come comrades, come
Lift up those jowls
With a mighty howl
Let the world delight
In the jewels on your face
For this is the place
To enjoy the art
And relish the poetry
Of those smiling faces
Standing in front of you

                                        6/25/2020 #4

Day-5 "Wonderful Ways"

Outside my window today
Little birds chirping away
What a wonderful way
To start my day

Their chirping
So happy and gay
Makes me wonder
What they say

Makes me want to fly away
Away up high
In the blue, blue sky
Away on a powder puff cloud

Catch a sunrise over the plains
Grab a rainbow while it rains
Put a flower in a vase
See the smile on your face

Little birds chirping away
Makes me happy and gay
What a wonderful way
To start my day

6/26/2020 #5

Last night as I lay sleeping it dawned on me that each poem is a pillar, or a bonding rivet, that when all is tied together, I would have a happy bridge. So, for the moment I decided to let it be so I could see what these poems would build. The question I have to answer is, will they be strong enough to breech the gap and hold the weight of those who pass. Will it truly be a bridge worthy of the name "Joy"?

Day-6 "Gifts"

This thing for you
I place it at your feet
A treasure from my soul
Is yours to keep

It is quite simple
Not coated in gold
Comes with a name
But has no fame

It has been scripted
A million times
Bled from the heart
It stands with time

It means that I care
That I want to share
The love I have
Only for you.

> *Thank You she replied*
> *There is no greater gift*
> *That I would desire*
> *It makes me happy and gay*

So simple these things
That I script
Come with a bow
For you to unfold

If, by chance, you discover
What lies inside
I'll treasure forever
And gift you more
For it makes me happy and gay

Lon 6/27/2020 #6

Day-6 "Mr. Bo Jangles and I"

As the early morning rays
Broke through the clouds
As if in a trance
I clicked my heels
And began to dance

The morning adrift in
Crisp mountain air
The freedom it brings
Implores that I sing
And jump through the sky

Spinning and twirling
Twisting and turning
Around the mountain I danced

Yellows and Purples
Reds and Oranges
Palettes of wildflowers
From the meadow below
On my canvas did fly

On this lofty plateau
In the crisp mountain air
We danced
To the script that grew
From a brush that flew
Mr. Bo Jangles and I   6/26/2020 #7

This poem is all about making/forcing yourself to feel good. Jump up and down and click your heels. Give it a try. It is quite invigorating. I did that this morning, and it really did make me feel good. And since I am writing about good and happy things setting the mood is critical to this task of 365. For whatever reason the song, "Mr. Bo Jangles" entered my brain.

Day-7 "Help"

Is a word that
Everybody needs
Every once in a while
It comes with a smile

It comes about
When you are in doubt
Reaches out
When you strikeout

When there is no place
For you to go
It gives you space
To uplift your face
It journeys from neighborhood doors
Swims oceans
Forges rivers
Crosses deserts
Lives in our hearts

Tell me
Who hasn't been gifted
By this word
Even if you have to ask.

It comes in a box
With a bow on top
Open it and you will find
The word I am talking about

"HELP"

6/28/2020 #8

Day-8 "Sunflower"

They greet the morning
With a smile
Pray with it
When it sets
Always a smile on their face

In fields and pastures
Roadsides and dusty trails
God's gift to all who pass
Leaving smiles for many miles

There is always one
Lords over the others
A kingly knight
Straight up and right
You want to own

I brought one home
One summer day
And placed it on my wall
Lords over all who enter now

I brought one home
One summer day
Plucked it from a store
Put it in a vase
Sits on a table in our hall

Gave one to my lover
One summer day
She held it in her arms
All winter long
She blessed me with a child

I sing to her now
You're the fairest of them all
My sweet "Sunflower"

                                                   6/29/2020 #9

Day-8 "Sail Away"

When all is gray
Grab a cloud
And Sail Away

Put a smile on your face
A sparkle in your eye
Spread your arms
And fly to places far away

Whistle with a song
As you rise to lofty heights
Touch the sky with your hands
Grab a piece of the sun
Put a star in your pocket
Kiss a rainbow
When raindrops fall

Let the wind blow you
Across the seas
Over mountain peaks
And frosty plains

Fly with cranes
On their northward way
Run with gazelles
On African plains
Sing with cockatoos
In Brazilian trees

Find a stone to sit upon
Listen to feathered voices
Babbling brooks and
Whispering winds

Just grab a cloud
And "Sail Away"   6/29/2020 #10

Day-9 "Here Comes the Sun"

Wake up darlings
The sun is breaking through
The frosty air has passed

The sun is coming
Smiles returning
Faces beaming
Forests greening

Time to celebrate
To congregate
To jubilate
To illuminate

It is time to
Swing in the trees
Twirl in the breeze
Sing with the bees
Share a frosty freeze

So happy to see
Your smiley face
This happy place
A flower in a vase
All covered in lace

Come darlings come
Here comes the sun
It's alright
Let's have some fun

6/30/2020 #11

I think it is a lot of fun to take lyrics from a song and incorporate them into a poem. Actually, when on my morning romp around the house, I watched the sun coming up and the shadows it was making, and I declared here comes the sun. I then began to sing "Here Comes the Sun" by the Beatles.

Day-9 "Pump it UP"

Shout it out!
Pump it up!
Pump it up!
Let's get this feeling right

Jump it up!
Jump it up!
Jump with all your might
Let's get this feeling right

Yell it out!
Yell it out!
Without any doubts
Let's get this feeling right

Clap!
Clap!
Clap your hands
Let's get this feeling right

Stomp!
Stomp!
Stomp your feet
Let's get this feeling right
Raise your arms
To the sky
Grab a friend
And shout it out
We gotta get this feeling right.

Pump it up!
Jump it up!
Yell it out!
Raise your arms to the sky
It will surely make you high

6/30/2020 #12

Day-10 "Imaginations"

Let's Waltz across the sky
Take a journey with the sun
See how far we fly
Before the evening comes

Let's Tango in Peru
With a lady from Kalamazoo
Frolic on a beach
On the Isle of Capri

Let's climb aboard
A Hip Hop bus
On its journey
Through Germany

Let's disco in Frisco
To forever Janis J.
Earth Wind and Fire
In old Santa Fe

Let's lay some stones
For others that may come
Leave our footprints in the sand
Take a journey with the sun
And dance away our fears

7/1/2020 #13

Day-10 "Alluring"

Oh, beautiful lady
You come to me
In midnight dreams
Traveling up and down my spine
Touching me in places
I have yet to know

Alluring thoughts I cannot hide
Awaken me in the morn
So beautiful,
               My darling
You by my side
That smile upon your lips

                                       7/1/2020 #14

Day-11 "Laying Stones and Building Bridges"

Let us celebrate
This "Happiness Day"
As we build the bridge of "Joy"
Over the "Valley of Despair"

Let's start with this rock
Let's place it here
Where all can see
A footing strong
Where there is no wrong

It is our corner stone
We'll name it "Love"
Blind to words unkind
A constant remind
It's laid in the mind

Let's sing "Joys" to this day
Rain "Praises" from our hearts
As we consecrate this stone
In the name of the gifter of love
On this "Happiness Day"

                                7/2/2020 #15

Remembering that my original objective was to create 365 poems of joy and happiness I felt that it is time to begin building this bridge over the "Valley of Despair". This is a battle that we all must overcome. I can already detect a difference in my thoughts, my happiness and actions.

Day-11 "Independence Day"

Freedom, freedom
That's our game
Let it ring out
Across our land

Courage, courage
That's our fame
Let us bring
The redcoats down

Liberty, liberty
That's our goal
Let our nation grow
Into a wondrous land

Equality, equality
What we desire
For all our peoples
For we are one

Let the bells ring
From steeples high
All across this land

Let's all cry out
It's "Independence Day"   7/2/2020 #16

My cheerleader poem with red, white and blue pom poms, of course.

Day-12 "Flowers"

Everywhere we look
They abound
In verses
And in rhymes

Valleys, meadows
Mountain brooks
Blue, blue skies and
Power puff clouds

Lavender and roses
Springtime charms
Paintings pictures
Little girl wishes

People places
Memories too
Plucked from places
You recall

Stories you've heard
Books you've read
Hiking trails and
Ocean shores

Mothers and daughters
Fathers and sons
Bedtime stories on
Stormy nights

Your lovers
And others
Spicy and hot
Some quite naughty
As you recall

Rock stars and steel guitars
Piccolos and Broadway shows
Castles on the Rhine
Journeys of the mind

Who said it has to be a star
Who is to deny
Your peace of mind
Yours to cherish
Call it what you want
They are flowers in your heart
And paintings on your wall

7/3/2020 #17

Flowers are Mother Nature's jewelry. They give color to life and spice to your soul. They bring light to darkness. They tease your brain and bring smiles to your face. Anything that brings a little color and spice to your life is a flower.......

Day-12 "Prayer"

There is just one thing
That I ask of you
Give me joy, Oh Lord,
Give me joy

There is just one thing
I ask of you
Grant me laughter, Oh Lord,
Grant me laughter

There is just one thing
I ask of you
Let me sing, Oh Lord,
Let me sing

There is just one thing
I ask of you
Give me a glad heart, Oh Lord,
Give me a glad heart.

For if I have a glad heart,
Oh Lord,
I will sing your praise
And laugh with the
Joy it brings to those
Lost souls
I meet along the way

7/3/2020 #18

Day-13 "Happy Days"

Today is the Happiest Day of my life.
The sun is shining brighter than I've ever known.
The sky is the brightest blue I've ever seen.
The grass is the greenest green I've ever tiptoed through.

Must you wonder why this is the Happiest Day of my life?
Would you be surprised if I told you why?
Would you think it can't be true?
Well, let me tell you something new.

Come rain or shine
Or our remaining time

When today becomes yesterday it will have been the
Happiest Day of my life.
When tomorrow becomes today it will be the
Happiest Day of my life.
When today becomes today it will be the
Happiest Day of my life.

Of course, there will be days when you cry and
There will be days when you sigh.
But you can choose, even in strife, how you live your day.
So let it be Merry and Gay. Let there always be a shining star
That you can put in your pocket no matter how far from Happy you are.

                         7/4/2020 #19

Day-13 "Happy Days-2"

Happy can be in a galaxy far away or as close as your bedroom door.
Happy can be staring out your window or playing with a child
Happy can be penning these words or singing out loud
Happy can be mourning a friend or cherishing a memory
Happy can be anywhere or anything you choose it to be; you just have to choose the Happy you want for today, for today is the only "DAY" you have. So find some
Happy in every "DAY" you have.

7/4/2020 #20

Day-14 "Simple Things"

What is it about simple things
That appeal to me
The scent of a rose
The shape of a cloud
The music of a flute
The rising and setting suns
Skipping stones on water's edge
A watch that is just a watch
A friendly touch
A "Thank You" when you're done

Why make it a task
Make it simple
And it will last

7/5/2020 # 21

Day-14 "Shared Moments"

Why make it complicated
She said
It's no more than a moment
Ours to enjoy.

                                                          7/5/2020 #22

Day 14 "Taking Advantage"

Jump up and down
Pluck that flower
From my hand
This moment
Is not long   7/5/2020 #23

Day 15 "Sacrifice"

What is there about this word
That makes it joyful?

Some would say that there is nothing
Joyful about this most uncommon of words
That is so little used.

Its use is a deed.
An action demanded.
Without question you do.
Gracious alms from your heart.

Sometimes a life is given
To save a life.

Sometimes an opportunity lost
When your baby is ill.

Sometimes someone else's hunger
Is greater than yours.

It is a choice you make
For a superior good.
It is bathed in love
From feelings inside.

It brings you inner peace
Without thought of reward.
You've saved a life.
Gave someone hope;
Fed a poor man of the street

A most precious thing,
Sharing with others,
Caring for others,
When you have nothing else to give.
Is a joy beyond compare
No reward required.

7/6/2020 # 24

I picked a word today that I felt needed a new spin. It often turns our emotions into raging torrents of hate. Sometimes we think that giving up something for someone else is not joyful. It can and often does make us angry. I gave this up because you wanted to do that? I'm stuck here and you are out there playing and having fun? What makes you think that your life or your desires are more important than mine?

I have tried to turn this word into the feelings/emotions you have when you have helped or done something for someone along your life's journey; when you had to give up something for their better good or wellbeing. There is Joy in those acts, and I truly mean Joy.

Day-16 "Stupid Confusion Makes Me Laugh"

While sitting on my porch one afternoon
A Sunday kind of day
I began to wonder why Sundays are called Sundays
Is it because there is sun in the day just like
There is a too in Tuesday or a wed in Wednesday?
How about a fry in Friday?
Who came up with these days anyway? And
Why couldn't there be more
More days to name
        Would make a great Game

I've heard they came from a mathematician in Brazil
But I think that is rather absurd. Why would a mathematician
In Brazil care to name the days in a week?
By the way, who discovered week?
And where was it hiding?
        There should be more weeks.

Contemplating souls often times have amusing thoughts
How absurd is that a wayward "he" soul replied?
I prefer to laugh and dance in the rain said another "she" soul.
For all practical purposes that could have been seashore
But why make it not rhyme because this is a Sunday?
Not a minute more shall I test my brain because
It is such a perfect day.
        There should be more days

A "mom" soul said. I think you should tickle yourself
A "dad" soul said, I think you need a drink
A "dog" soul said, scratch my neck
Who am I to complain; I'll do all three.
My brain won't know the difference.
Besides that, it is a Sun---- day kinda day
The funnest day of my life.
        There should be more days

                        7/7/2020 #25

Day-16 "There Comes a Time"

There comes a time
To lay down roots
Discover your true Love
Raise flowers in your master suite
Teach your offspring
How to sing
Play a guitar on a swing

There comes a time
For you to listen
When she says that you are wrong
That you will be forgiven
If you can pen a rhyme

There comes a time
To be funny
When rain is pounding on your door
And she in another room
As you hide behind the couch
In a lion's crouch.

There comes a time
To take a flower from the field
Let its perfume fill your room
Bath in Lilacs
Naked on the floor

There comes a time
To praise the Lord
For what he has given
And not what has been taken

There comes a time
To rest your limbs
For the hills that you have climbed
The stories that you have writ
The places you have known

There comes a time
To end these lines
And laugh with all
Who've drank your wine
While dancing in your mind

7/7/2020 #26

Day-17 "Have you forgotten"

I watched a little girl
Pink bow in her hair
Skipping down the street
Playing hopscotch on the walk
Never missing an empty space
It brought a smile to my face
Have you forgotten how to hop?

I watch a little boy
Playing with his toys
Skipping rocks across the pond
Having so much fun
Chasing silly geese
It brought a smile to my face
Have you forgotten how to skip?

I watched a young mother
Push her carriage filled with two
Down a tree laden path
A bonnet on her head
Singing a heavenly melody
It brought a smile to my face
Have you forgotten how to love?

I watched a young man
Getting on a bus
Headed somewhere west
Baseball cap on his head
Whistling a corny tune
It brought a memory back
I have yet to forget.
It brought a smile to my face

                                                7/8/2020 #27

Day-17 "Have You Forgotten-2"

Have you forgotten how to skip
As little girls do
Be a princess in a midnight dream?

Have you forgotten how to jump up high
And click your heals.
Be Bo Jangles in a country tune?

Have you forgotten how to dance
Without a band
Just you and her on seaside sand?

Have you forgotten how to sing
A crazy song
As it floats across your brain?

Have you forgotten how to count
When it's your due
At a dinner for two?

Have you forgotten how to touch
Your lovers spot
When she cries for more?

Have you forgotten how to smile
No matter the time or day
No matter who or where
No matter what or why?

Have you forgotten how to skip?

7/8/2020 #28

Day-17 "Sunflowers"

Who are the sunflowers
In your life?
Sons and daughters
Little ones in the way?

Friends and lovers
Teachers and preachers
Saints and mothers too?

Times and trials
Places and things
Sunny days and candle lights?

Fields of flowers
Turning with the sun
From dawn to evening tide?

They can be
Anything that brings
A fond memory from the past
A smile to your face

That is why we place
Sunflowers in our days
And in our many plays

7/8/2020 #29

Day-17 "Caring"

As we gaze across these oceans wide
And from these mountain peaks
Think of all there is to see

As we sit beside these babbling brooks
Gazing up at stars
In our nations parks
Think of all there is to share

As we hike these many trails
Breathing in the misty air
Etching in the memory
The beauty of these hallowed spaces

The lakes and waterfalls
That lie along our paths

The deer and elk
In pastoral scenes

Thunderheads
Rising in the west

Bumble bees
And hummingbirds
Singing in the breeze

Just think!

Think of all there is to see
Think of all there is to share
Think of all there is to be
If we only care.

      "We have to care"

                        7/8/2020 #30

Day-18 "Sprinkling Sunshine"

A feathered friend
Came humming about last night
Touching the flowers in our
Garden space.

Dashing and darting
From petal to petal
Stamen to stamen
As tough he were in heaven

In and out his
Needle nose pierced
Searching for the
Nectar within

Consumed by the
Intoxicating blend
Of perfumes and sugars
Of insane beauty and dreams
He couldn't resist
He came and went
And back for more

Little he knew
He was furthering the rise
Of life's everlasting voyage
We the happy recipients
Of this lustful scene
Played out in our
Garden space.

Thank you my
Tiny, feathered friend
For the simplest of things
For sprinkling a little sunshine
In our Garden space.   7/9/2020 #31

Day-18 "Sprinkling Sunshine on Your Flowers"

When you have a friend in doubt
Give him a slap on the back
Put him on the right track

When she thinks no one else cares
Give her a hug and
Tickle her toes

When your eyes are full of tears
Wash away those fears
With a smile on your face

When it is all gloomy
And rainy outside
Open your eyes to the beauty
It will bring

There is always something good
In all that we see
In all that we do
For all those we care

Life is full of flowers
Enamor them with sunshine
And they will glow

7/9/2020 #32

Day-18 "Sharing Stars"

When you are happy and gay
Reach in your pocket
Pull out a star and
Give it to a friend

Stars are shining emblems
That brighten the midnight hours
Admired is the man
Who cheerfully shares his stars

There are plenty
To go around
But sometimes they are missing
From someone you care
Who needs an uplifting

Happy is the child
Who receives a star
Its kindness repaid
With a memory
Far away from now

They all have names
When sharing them
Let your friend know
Who they are

I give to you this day "Joy"
For it is a wonderful way
To spend the day

I give to you this day "Serenity"
For everything is right
It's such a beautiful sight

From my pocket
I give to you this day "Hope"
Even as the wind blows
There is no reason to mope

Reach deep inside
I give you this day "Kindness"
It is the smoothest one
It will show you how to shine

This one is "Admiration"
My gift to you this day
For others more talented
Than you

I named this one "Cheerful"
Because it has a funny shape
And laughs at all I do
It even knows how to tie its shoes

There are many, many more
That I will save for another day
When you have the time
To sit with me awhile.

7/9/2020 #33

Day-19 "Discovering Beauty"

This ol' world has beauty to give
If we only look around

There is beauty in the rising sun
When it peaks above the crown

In majestic clouds
On their journeys across the sky

In golden rainbows
In heavenly arcs

In budding flowers
After springtime showers

In hummingbirds
And buzzing bees

In waving wheat
On rolling hills

Bubbling brooks
And cascading falls

White mountain peaks
And pounding waves
On ocean shores

Forests of yellows and oranges
In October cloth

There is beauty in the setting sun
When it slips beyond the crown.

She has plenty to give
Of her beauty all around   7/10/2020 #34

Day-20 "Trust"

This poem came about because our president commuted the sentence of Roger Stone yesterday. It is hard for me to believe that any president of this country would be so arrogant as to undermine justice I'm sorry for letting my emotions loose today, but "trust" is such an important word. We must have trust in both our fellow men and our political systems, if not we fall into that pitiful pit of anarchy.

Building this bridge
This bridge of "Joy"
Over the "Valley of Despair"
Will undoubtedly challenge
The moral fiber of our being

The hardships employed
Are to be enjoyed
For our purpose is much greater
Our reward more blessed

Trust your fellow man
When he lends a hand
As we bridge the gap
Between hate and love

Who said it would be easy
To bridge this "Valley of Despair"
It is not for the faint
But for the strength of conviction

Imagine the end
Our goal we will defend
This daunting task
Will surely test

Rise up, Rise up
Put a song in your soul
Cast from this air
All thoughts of despair

"Trust"

The stone
We lay today.

                              7/11/2020 #35

Day-20 "Sometimes"

Sometimes,
I just want to be a better human
It is not an illusion
Surrounded in confusion

Not an easy task
But must confess
A package I want to undress

Sometimes, when in doubt
My stomach tied in knots
I want to have happy thoughts

Not an easy task
When insanity reigns
And thunder pores like rain

Sometimes, I want to share love
With someone in need
I feel it's my deed

Not an easy task
When they scream
As if in a dream

Sometimes, I want to laugh
At the silly things you do
When you're in a stew

Not an easy task
When the shoe you toss
Hits me in the ass

Sometimes,
I just want to be a better human
It's not an easy task

                        7/11/2020 #36

Day-21 "Anticipation"

The car is packed
There is no going back
New sights to see
Wherever they may be
Joyful my adventurous soul
Tomorrow I leave
My destiny unfolds

I'm Christopher sailing the sea
Glen flying across the sky
Lewis crossing the great divide
An adventure, no longer a dream
My heart ready to scream

Let loose the cord that
Binds the boat
Break champagne across my bow
Untie the reins that hold my stead
I'm high and ready to say goodbye

Tomorrow is my day
An amazing dream
The joy it will bring

The car is packed
I'm ready to go.

7/12/2020 #37

This poem came about as I was preparing to photograph flowers in the American Basin near Lake City, Colorado. It's about the joy of anticipating the journey. We all have events/journeys that we dream about. Believe it or not sometimes this is the greatest Joy.
Why not enjoy it......

Day-21 "Balloons"

Rising high up in the sky
Floating on a breeze
Men in bubbles fly

Floating on a breeze
Meadows far below
Landscapes that really please

Meadows far below
Serenity to your soul
Drifting like the snow

Serenity to your soul
Early morning light
Ink upon your scroll

Early morning light
Daisies in the sky
Such a beautiful sight

Daisies in the sky
Floating on a breeze
Men in bubbles fly   7/12/2020 #38

Day-22 "Rocky Roads"

Rocky roads are up ahead
A voice inside me said
Without a doubt
You're sure to be tested

The mountain peak
Is beyond your reach
You haven't the strength
To attain that height
The courage to have that right

Forgive me if I think
Your bones too frail
Your muscles to weak
Your mind too meek

So, what, my heart replied
You don't know the grit I hide
The pride inside

As sure as the sun will rise
That mountain I'll breech

For there are flowers in the vale
That are within my reach
Each one I'll kiss and
Drink of its perfume
With each sip, I'll thirst for more

Before I'm through
That mountain will fall
It is no more than a rock in the road.

7/13/2020 #39

This poem came to me while driving to the American Basin near Lake City, Co. It was the rockiest road I've ever been on. However, the thought of seeing those mountain flowers drove me on.

Day-23 "Waterfall"

What will I see today?
The sun rising over a fall
A trail that's not too hard
An adventure never had
Something I've never seen
Something I've never tried

A chance encounter
A challenge never conquered
A surprise for my bucket
A joy I have yet to hold

What's on the other side?
You'll never know
Until you crest the hill.

                                                      7/13/2020 #40

North Clear Creek Falls between Creed and Lake City, Co.

Day-23 "Joys"

Joys are like toys
Full of colors, sights and sounds
Yellows, reds and blues

They come wrapped in boxes
With ribbons and bows.

They are sparkling eyes and
Little girl smiles

They can be little or large
A peck on the cheek
An ocean you've sailed

Playing catch with your son
Sledding on a snowy day

Tossing balls
Chasing sticks
A puppy by your side

Words you've writ
Songs you've sung
Places you've been

Moments shared
Moments loved
Joys you'll put away
For a rainy day

7/13/2020 #41

Day-24 "Amazing"

Have you ever caught a
Sunset before it fell?

Have you ever searched
For love on a rainy day?

Have you ever held a snowflake
Before it turned to rain?

Have you ever skipped a rock
That would not sink?

Have you ever kissed a girl
Before she asked you to?

Have you ever played hopscotch
With the lady next door?

Have you ever written a poem
To give as a gift?

Have you ever held a door
For someone much older than you?

Have you ever built a castle
Just to watch it wash away?

Have you ever sang a song
That would not end?

There are so many evers
I could go on forever

Remind me to save a few
For the next forever day
That comes my way.   7/14/2020 #42

Day-24 "Snaps and Snips"

Snaps and snips are like trinkets; they mean nothing for they are the opposite of reality. Every once in a while, you need to do a reality check. So, the idea is to write something that is absolutely insanely stupid. It's soul food to your idiotic imagination. I have written a numerous number of these whenever I need to charge my batteries. They are just fun to do..... So here goes with a few.

I cannot lie
I am not pure
I swear
That empty wine bottle
On the table just winked at me

I thought it quite funny
That I am not funny
I would rather be a bunny
Than a dummy

I must confess
That I am a mess
My arms are longer than my legs
My toes much longer than my fingers
My eyes much larger than my ears
My thing much.........
My oh my if only I could fly

That bridge is so tall that
My boat can't sail over
That river so wide that
My plane can fly under

I want to be a movie star
So, I won't have to wear clothes
And be known for my bare closet
And it's 1,000 shoes

I want to be a rodeo clown
And jump in a barrel
With a six pack of beer

I want to be an ocean wave
Who never finds a shore

I could do more of these stupid snaps but
I swear that stupid wine bottle just
Winked at me again....

Cheers.

7/14/2020 #43

Day-25 "Reminisce"

Come back------ Come back
A voice kept calling

NO-----NO
Yes-----Yes

You must not forget
The clock turned back
The times we loved

You said we would keep
It forever and a day
You kissed my cheek
No holding back

We danced in the flowers
Made love in the rain
Wrote notes to each other
In the evening hours
Sailed across the ocean
On a magic cloud

Held hands as we walked
Down the aisle

NO-----NO
Yes-----Yes

It all comes back
Perfume to my brain
Your sweet nectar on my lips
I care not to miss
This reminisce

Yes-----Yes----Yes--Yes

                                        7/15/2020 #44

Day-25 "Trails"

Trails, Trails
And
More Trails

Where they lead
Is unknown

What differences
Does it make

Just choose

You will find
Your way
Eventually

With gladness in your heart
And
A smile upon your face

You'll know
You
Did it your way

Choosing your own trail
Is
What matters

More than
Anything else

                              7/15/2020 #45

Day-25 "Trials"

Rocky trails and Muskrat tales
Are gifts from heaven
Though they are laden
With many a trial

A rocky trail is filled
With bumps and bruises
But a Muskrat tale
Enlightens the soul

When you slip and fall
Grab hold the tale
For the Muskrat knows
You cannot fail
To find the
Wondrous Joys
Bequeathed to you

When you master
A rocky trail.   7/15/2020 #46

Day-25 "The Farmer Said"

Like the farmer said
You gotta make hay
When the hay is right

So, I picked up my fork
And began to pitch

Like the poet said
You gotta write
When the feeling is right

So, I picked up my pen
And began to write   7/15/2020 #47

Day-25 "Little Squirrel"

Tree to tree
Branch to branch
The little guy jumped

Like a trapezist
He flew through the air
With the greatest of ease

Across the forest lawn
He scampered
Running from tree to tree

It was really a sight to see
For he was quite the tease
Crazy drunk on glees

I don't believe he cared
As I watched from afar
He just wanted to please
With the greatest of ease   7/15/2020 #48

Day-27 "Silly Day"

Let's make it silly
Like a Jack in the Box
Kind of day
Surprise! Surprise!
What hides inside?

His name is really Willy
Not Willy Nilly
As you implied

Let's turn the world upside down
Fly a kite over the Rhine
Punch the sky
With a sigh
Never asking why
Just wave goodbye

Bye little birdie
Way up in the sky
I've always wanted to fly
Especially when I'm high

Do you think I could fly
If I tried?

You silly old man
Don't you know
It takes a plan
If you want to fly like me

To which I replied
Surprise, Surprise
My name is not Billy
It is really Willy

I come from a box
And I can jump really high
Would you like to see me try?
I just want to be silly

7/16/2020 #49

Day-28 "Dancing in the Street"

Dancing in the street
Is really quite a treat
Swaying to the beat
Is really quite neat

Turn up the sound
Make it pound
Twirl around
Jump off the ground

Some will say you are crazy
But who cares if you are little hazy
It means you're not lazy
When you shine like a daisy

So many un-smiles
Go on for miles
Like sundials
Left in piles

It's time to let loose
Fly like a goose
Strip off the noose
Don't be a recluse

It's not a big deal
To strip and peal
It's like a great meal
It has a great feel

Without a doubt
Let it hang out
There is no doubt
In the song you flout

It is really quite neat
To dance in the street

7/17/2020 #50

Day-28 "Searching"

Where have they gone?
I've looked every where
In concrete canyons
In grassy meadows
Behind closed doors
Nowhere to be found

Some say here
Same say there
Please tell me
Where have they gone?

I want them back
Put on the right track
My mouth agape
They were my Prozac
Where have they gone?

The green in the valley
The blue in the sky
The rain in the forest
The bees on leaves
Where have they gone?

I ask you please
For what are these
But wildflowers
Rising at my feet

7/17/2020 #51

You can search everywhere for good thoughts or smiles yet so many times they are lying right in front of you.

Day-28 "Sparkles"

What are they but
Little bright lights
Brightening your nights
Pan pipe notes
Floating across the sky

A good deed
A gracious thank you
A wondrous praise
A funny little note
An ice cream cone

Someone you love
An old friend
A neighbor
A daughter or a son
Your forever mate

A pleasure
A treasure
A leisure
A piece of apple pie

A smile
A kind word
A hearty laugh
A well told joke
A glass of red wine

The sun shining through
Your boudoir pane
The musky scent of
Last night's love

7/17/2020 #52

Day-29 "So Proud"

Talk to me oh page
Spill your thoughts
Let them fall
From my pen

I read you today
Oh Langston Hughes
Your words touched my soul
Simplistic is your pen
Such knowledge I respect

We lost you today
Dear John
A man of supreme courage and grit
And bloodied brow

We lost you today
Dear C.T.
A man of supreme courage and grit
Sprawled on the steps by Sheriff John Clark

I've walked that bridge
Shed tears with you
Little I know
The pain you've endured

I am white
And am not black
Why is the ink on this page
So black today?

I cannot mask my pain
It is not my most favorite day

But I will smile
And hold my hand high

So proud am I
We've had men like these

                        7/18/2020 #53

Reflections on the passing of John Lewis and C.T. Vivian. Two of the greatest civil rights leaders of our era.

Day-29 "Convictions"

Hold fast the cup
You dip in the garden of hope
Don't let it steal the trust
You hold in your heart
For your fellow man

Take hold the rope
You lower into the well of knowledge
Don't let them steal the words
You hold in your heart
For the things you need to say

Raise high the ladder
You place against the wall of justice
Don't let them steal the scales
For all are equal
In the name of our law

Overflow the vessel of peace
You keep in your heart
Don't let their troubled spirts hold you down
Hold your arm high
With a smile on your face

Dress your tree of love
With gifts from your soul
Give all who pass
A hearty hello

Pull from the river of kindness
The gratitude you have for
All you have to be thankful for

       7/18/2020 #54

Day-30 "Alluring-2"

A word that drew me near
Found on Capri
Full of dreams
And enticing themes

A most mysterious word
Uncommonly used
That I rarely hear
It drew me near

A most beautiful word
Undefined by many
Difficult to describe
It drew me near

A most elusive word
Different things to many
Some never find
It drew me near

A most mythical word
Kings and knights
Little boy dreams
It drew me near

A word of many poets
Tracing their words
On scented scrolls
It drew me near

A most loving word
When you discover
You can't live without
She drew me near

       7/19/2020 #55

Day-31 "Good O Boys and their Toys"

They came squealing by in
Twenty-nines and Fifty-nines
Thirty-twos and Sixty-fives
Camaros and Birds
Dusters and Goats
Vets and old army jeeps

Each with a tale
Harder to believe
Each time it was told
Years of practice turned old

Hot dates on Saturday nights
Hotter dates in back door seats
High school rings for a kiss
Letter jackets for a little more

Saturday night
Main Street drag
Honking horns and squealing tires
Who's that pretty girl from southern Cal?
Names like Piston and Dip Stick
Troubles and Pin head

Doc and Ernie
Hey Jimbo, how's your differential?

Blowing smoke and leaking oil
Clanging pistons and screaming belts
Chrome wheels and no seat belts
Blowers and fake Ids
Hey, would you guys buy me a six pack
The good sheriff drove me home...

7/20/2020 #56

Day-31 "THE "COFFEE CUP" CAFÉ"

The theme of this poem is that silent moment when no one has or can say anything; they are so amazed they cannot speak. I am having coffee with these old car nuts who meet for coffee every Monday morning at the Coffee Cup Café in Monument, Colorado.

The Coffee Cup Café
Where all things happen
And nothing else is new
Old men sit and chatter
Around a table fit for knights

Steaming brews in hand
Filled by sultry girl
In sculpted jeans
Flirting for dimes
Bacon grease in the air

Muffler heads and wing nuts
Of by gone era
Thirty-two's and forty-eight's
Sometimes a 57
Stored in garages
Massaged by hands
Of velvet steel
Cruising and hot rods

Their prime desire
Gasoline and oil
The bond that bolts
Them together

The love of their lives
Mary Lou & Bobby Sue
V8's and cleavage
All fender benders
Always broken
Always a lie

There was a dumbfounding moment one day
For these old muffler heads and wing nuts
Fuel injectors and baseball caps
When out of the blue
A question was asked of one,
What are you doing today?

Their eyes popped
Their jaws dropped
Coffee spewed out of their mouths
The cutie pie flipped a tray
A lug wrench dropped
And hit the floor

Their tires no longer burned
Their gaskets blown
Their headers exploded

Deadly silence

I'm doing a poetry reading at three
Would you like to come?

                                                      7/20/2020 #57

Day-32 "Word of the Day"

Hold it in your hand
Let its touch heal your anxiety
It has a nice ring
It rhymes with divinity

Inhale the fragrance
Of its wonder
Let it baptize your soul
It rhymes with contentedly

Seize the breeze
That rustles the leaves
Of galaxies far
It rhymes with eternity

Capture a sunset
In Yosemite
Savor its glow
It rhymes with heavenly

Play a flute
On a grassy knoll
Let the sheep know your call
It rhymes with breathlessly

Wrap your arms
Around her
Tell her you love her
It rhymes with ecstasy

Gift yourself this word
Joyful its peace
Beautiful its tranquility
Is but

"Serenity"   7/21/2020 #58

Day-32 "Pillars of Peace"

I ventured back to the valley today
To see if I could lay more stones
To bridge the "Valley of Despair"

Sitting on the edge of the cliff
Was an old man who asked what I was doing.
I replied, building a bridge over this valley I call "Despair"
Through which a raging river flows
It is to be called "Joy"

What a formidable task; the old man replied.
The gap you intend to bridge is long
It appears you have only begun.
What will you use for pillars

To which I replied.
My pillars are peace
Allow me to explain

The foundation was laid with Love
Upon which I will place
Goodness and gentleness
Faithfulness and humility
Happiness and tranquility
Justice and human rights
Respect and good will
Calmness and serenity

All these and many more
Will support the iron of "Joy"

Once all the peace is placed
I'll lay the iron that will
Stretch to the other side

There upon the old man rose
And with a twitch of his eye asked
What is it you wish to find
On the other side?

As I recall, I told the old man.
That will have to wait
For another day.   7/21/2020 #59

There are many types and kinds of peace. The thought is that if you find peace, both inward and outward, you find joy and that is indeed a most difficult task.

Day-33 "An Ode to a Beauty"

She took my breath away
Her sleek lines
Her flowing mane
Kentucky bred

I saw her as a child
Her eyes of sparkling diamonds
Tall and slender her body of steel
A beauty beyond compare

I saw her as a lady
Dark bronzed skin
Sleek and ravishing
A body to melt the souls of men

I saw her as a woman
Anxious for love
A winner beyond description
A champion who never lost

Galloping across the
Green meadows of my mind
She never fails to
Win my eye

The beauty she is
Her sleek dark body
Resting in the green grass
Of the Kentucky hills
"Zenyatta" her name

Zenyatta was a thoroughbred racehorse known as the Queen of Racing. She won 19 consecutive races in her three-year career. She was retired in 2010 after her 20th race at Churchill Downs where she took second. I love the name "Zenyatta"

7/22/2020 #60

Day-34 "Rewind"

My mind was a river that
Did not flow
A sun refusing to shine
A moon without a glow
No twinkling stars
No rhyming lines

Then all at once
From out of the dust and muck
On my cluttered desk
Jumped a tiny man
With bells on his toes
A jester's cap upon his crown

Crossing his legs on my pad
He squeaked Rewind
Rewind, you fool, Rewind!
Where upon he jumped and began
Flipping the pages of my pad
Until he came to where I began this journey
This journey of 365 journeys
He then squeaked, Read
Read, you fool, Read

Stunned, I began to Read
And read some more

It was then I discovered that
These readings made me happy
My mind began to skip and jump
Flip and flop and sing and dance

Then all at once
The tiny little man jumped up
Clicked his heels and off my pad he flew
Leaving traces of star dust on my pen

As if on cue
The clouds departed
The sun began to shine
The moon began to glow
The stars began to twinkle
The river began to flow
I found my "Rewind"

7/23/2020 #61

This thought came to me this morning when the word "Rewind" came into my mind. Needless to say, my thoughts were clouded over. So, anyway, I opened this book and began reading from the beginning. It was then I realized that these poems did indeed make me happy. The point is that sometimes we just need to retrace our journeys while awaiting the next journey that is sure to come.

Day-35 "Sashay"

Just think the word, Sashay
Let it meander through your brain

Say the word, Sashay
The many ways it means

Imagine the word, Sashay
See it drifting by

Take a stroll with, Sashay
Hold it in your hands

A name I would give my child
It has a beautiful ring, Sashay

Thoughts drifting across my mind
Memories of the Louvre
Just me and Sashay

Let it trace stars in your brain
Let it pluck from the heavens
Its beautiful tone
You can't help but love

"Sashay"

7/24/2020 #62

Day-35 "Wonders"

So many in this world
Too many to name
So many to entertain
The many wonders of this world

Some made by the hand of man
Mona Lisa's and Redeemers
China's Wall and Taj Mahal
Coliseums and Pyramids

Some by nature's hand
Barrier Reef and Victoria Falls
Grand Canyon and Mount Everest
Halong Bay the Blue Hole in Belize

The Wonders of this world
Will one ever know them all?
Will one ever see them all?

Some say Virtual Reality
Will solve it all.

Won't that be fun?
Sometimes I wonder how

7/24/2020 #63

Day-36 "Running"

Running here
Running there
Running, Running, Running,

Running for fame
It is a game
A treasure to claim

Running for gold
Just to hold
But it's really cold

Running to work
I'm just a clerk
For the upstairs jerk

Running to save
I am a slave
The way I behave

Running for change
Sounds really strange
I must rearrange

Running for good
If I could
I only would

Running for peace
Takes many pieces
Builds masterpieces

Running for justice
Without getting busted
You have to be trusted

Running to keep sane
Without claim
No one to blame

Running for Joy
A heart full of toys
Baskets of noise

Running for love
With a morning dove
Pens words of truelove

Running for fun
Don't be the one
Who says you won

It seems we're always running
Running here and
Running there

Why don't we just walk
To the park today
And watch little girls play
On merry go rounds and teeter tots

7/25/2020 #64

Day-36 "A Day in the Park"

Merry go rounds
        And
                Teeter tots

Round and round
Up and down

Jumping on
Jumping off

Bouncing up
Bouncing down

Little boys laughing
Little girls squealing

Mommies and daddies smiling
Grandmas and grandpas grinning

Watching for hours
As little ones play.
On merry go rounds
        And
                Teeter tots.

                                    7/25/2020 #65

Day-37 "My Palm Tree"

Upon my wall
There hangs a tree
Garnished in orange
The setting sun

It stood there
Tall and strong
That eve in May
The ocean strong

I had to have
That pristine scene
Mine alone
No other would I allow

To steal it would be a sin
But I put it in my pocket with a grin
To place upon my wall
When times turn grim

It bought me peace
That summer's eve
As I walked along
This sea shore scene

I'm sure it was the one
That swept the street
Where Jesus walked

I love it more each passing day
As I remember well
When I put it in my pocket with a grin

       7/26/2020 #66

Is but a memory from the past when we spent a couple of weeks on the Isle of Palms near Charleston, SC in 2018

Day- 37 "Why"

Tell me men of earth
Why you reach for stars
When all you have to do
Is put a smile upon your face
And give a little love from your heart
       7/26/2020 #67

Thought came from the poem "Question" by Robert Frost

Day- 38: "I Drew a Blank"

Somewhere a flower was lost
It pained my soul
The resolve it took
To put a smile on my face

                         7/28/2020 #68

Day-39 "Lost But Not Lost"

Searching, Searching, Searching
Where in space did it venture?
It's lost
Who stole this flower of mine?
It's gone

The vast galaxy of my mind
Could not recall
When it was taken
The moment it was lost
The name it was given
From the soil it was penned

A hurricane of frustration
Splashing at my soul
Tearing me limb from limb
Drowning my pen

A tsunami of Pacing
Pacing, Pacing
Back and Forth, Back and Forth
Across a river full of despair
Faltering, falling,
Slipping and stumbling
Nearly drowning

A quest to recapture
A flower I so deeply loved

An Avalanche of Whys
Why, Why?
Why this mind
Cannot recall
Where it fell or
Why it fell

She said
Give it some space
It's not lost
It's merely misplaced
Please slow your pace

Once more across
That river of despair I waded
And there upon the shore a bottle lay
A note within

Written there upon
A simple statement read
Open pages past
You will surely find the
Answer to your quest

Flipping back the pages
Of my mind
I came to Flower Twenty-nine
Then I recalled that
Yesterday a caisson came bearing
John Lewis across the Alabama River
Where he once lay beaten and bloodied

"So Proud" So Proud am I
We've had a man like this
My mind has cleared
My pen is spilling over

I found my flower
And knew what I had to do   7/28/2020 #69

Yesterday my mind was a total blank. I had lost the poem that is at the center of this poem. I searched everywhere I could think; in my trash, through every page of this book and every piece of paper on my desk, not once but numerous times. Totally frustrated, I went to bed without writing a single word. My wife kept telling me it was not lost and that I should look some more.

Upon waking this morning, I started all over and began to read the poems from my most recent past. It was there, that I found poem # 52 from Day-29. "So Proud". Somewhere, hidden in the depths of my mind was a lesson. It's that we must resolve to never lose sight of the struggle and persistence it demands of us all to overcome discrimination that men like John Lewis and C.T. Vivian fought and died for. So Proud am I of these men.

Day-40 "Topless"

Stripping her clothes
She lifts her arms to the sky
From mountain top high

The sun at her back
The valley below bright with green
The cool mountain air
Tingles her skin

Snap it quick
I'm shivering with delight .
You dared me to do it
I find it exciting

Spiritual freedom
Being naked with the sky
Not a soul around
Only the mountains see

Physically exhilarating
The path to this place
Stony, and treacherous
A post card reward for
The peril she endured

To stand here with
My back to the lenses
My breasts basking
In the cool mountain air

I cannot deny the
Freedom I feel.
The reward I've chased
To this mountain top high.

Snap it quick.
I may not want to go back.

7/29/2020 #70

This poem come from and article in the Colorado Springs, Co. Gazette. The article is about women who finish a hike by stripping off their shirts and then taking a photo of their back side. Interesting, what a great way to end your hike. I love it.

Day-41 "Leave Us With A Smile"

Printing your brain
Would drive most insane
Some would place you in jail
And bury the key

Others may enjoy an invite
And
Jump right in
Riding your waves
On a pink submarine

In the end
It's up to you
Rather you print or hide
All that's inside

But you will never know
Until you give it a try.

I hope it leaves you with a smile

7/30/2020 #71

Day-42 "Calling All"

Why aren't we writing
Happy rhymes?
Have we displaced our souls?

Is there so much wrong
We cannot see the sun?

Is the well so deep
We can't crawl out?

Is our humor a virus
We cannot light?

Our love of life
A candle without a wick?

I've read your many words
It pales my heart to think
We have to cry
Shed tears for our lives

What is wrong?
The tunnel so long
There is no light?

The death of a soul
Who shouldn't have passed?

I swore I wouldn't
Write an unkind rhyme

No matter the crime
There is still good in every day

Dig deep into your souls
My poetic friends

I'm sure you can find the time
To put a little "Happy" in your pen

Shout out your sorrow
Let it fly away

Man was not made for this and
Neither was I

7/31/2020 #72

It dawned on me this morning that I am getting tired of reading new verses that are filled with sorrow. I am getting tired of hearing all the unhappy news the press is telling. I am tired of our leaders defying the truth and expecting us to believe it. I am tired of all the hate on our city streets. I am tired of all the tear gas spewing from cans by camouflaged men. The boys and girls in border cages. I'm sick and tired of those who haven't the decency to wear a mask when in a crowd. I think it insane that we have stooped this low.

So, this is my call for all you poets to think good thoughts every once in a while. At least once a day. I realize that there is a lot of sorrow out there; that the convergences of police brutality, a deadly virus, lost souls in border cages, hot summer nights, and a leader who spews hate and stupid shit has created this reality. However, we poets and authors of script must not succumb to all this darkness. We cannot let this darkness rule our lives. That we must look to our faith, to our hope and our love that this world will change. That the faith, hope and charity that lies within each and every one of us will wash away our tears and fears. There is still a lot of life to live, and we need to celebrate that. So, I am encouraging all of you to take a few minutes each day and write something good. Be it a line or a short verse. Just do it. It will make you feel much, much better. And, yes it will make me feel much better as well.

Day-42 "Turn the Music Up"

Beat those drums

Strum those guitars.

Blow the socks off your sax

Pound those keys

Blow those pipes

Make your violin zing

Blow out your lungs

On that trombone

Stroke your pen

Let it spew "Happy"

All over your page

Turn the Music Up!

7/31/2020 #73

Day-42 "Set the Stage"

Set the stage for the music in your life

Open your curtains for all to see

Turn up the microphone

Call the maestro to the stage

Put the cymbals in their place

Tap the magic in your soul

Put a glorious beat in your heart

Dedicate your life to something whole

Play it higher than you can climb

Let it be happy and gay

Let it be lively and witty

Fill the stages of your life

With the music in your soul

Let your music set the stage

For all those who venture through

7/31/2020 #74

Day-43 "Let's Take A Walk"

I Think I will go
Walk around the earth today
To see if anyone is there
To see if anyone cares
To share a few laughs
To catch a few stars
To find a new place
To dream a dream
To sing a song
To play a play
To see a sea
To catch that cow
Who jumped over the moon
And the mouse who ran up the clock
Won't that be fun?

Would you like to come along?

8/1/2020 #75

Day-43 "The Gardener"

Who is the man
Who waters your soul

Tills the earth
To give you life

Plants the seeds
That feed your spirit

Fertilizes the soil
In your mind

Mows the weeds and
Keeps your furrows straight

Trims and plucks
The flowers in your garden place

Harvests the fruit
On your vine

Brings flowers to your table
When you are sad

He abides outside
But lives within

He's never one to hide
He's always by your side

You choose the path you take
The one He's cared for most

He is the Spirit in your soul
The Gardener of your life

8/1/2020 #76

Day-43 "Here's To"

A table for two
Two glasses of wine
Two roses for her
Two lovers holding hands

Two babies in a crib
                              Oh Crap!

Raise your glass
To the man who
Makes you laugh
As the wine within
Spills on your white blouse
                              That Sucks!

Don't you know
It is a sin
To drink a gin
Without a him
                              Screw it!

Don't you know
That when he cries
He can't explain why
It didn't rise
                              Good God!

Thank God it's Friday
And time to go home.
I promise to be sane
Come Monday morn.

Hey you there!

Turn off those friggin lights.

                                            8/1/2020 #77

Day-44 "My New Name"

Am gonna change
My name today
Think I'll make it "Fun"

Not Funny, Funnier nor Funnest
Just plain old "Fun"

Have you ever thought
What would be your fame
If you had a funny name?
For one, you would always be rich
That would be pretty cool

Just think, when someone calls
You say, "Fun" here

What they gonna say?
What's up "Fun"
Or Hey "Fun"
You wanna go have some fun

Have you ever thought about
Changing your name?

It's like, whenever you need a spark
Or having a trying day.
Just change your name.
What the hell!

What do you think about
"Happy", Happier or Happiest?
You will never know until you try it on

Today my name is "Fun"

8/2/2020 # 78

Day-44 "Word of the Day"

There is a word

I love to speak

I snared it from the sky

I noticed it never cries

I've seen it in lover's eyes

I've felt it on spring like days

I've savored it on a summer's eve

I've swam in its perfume

I've drank of its wine

I've drowned in its beauty

Made love on a

Feathered bed

"Fantastic"

8/2/2020 #79

Day-45 "I Don't Know"

Where would you like to go?
I don't know

What would you like to do?
I don't know

What do you want for dinner?
I don't know

Would you like a beer?
I don't know

Who called?
I don't know

Whose thing is that?
I don't know

Did you lose your phone?
I don't know

Did you lose your keys?
I don't know

Who spilled the wine?
I don't know

Who slept in my bed?
I don't know

Where did it go?
I don't know

Where did she go?
I don't know

Whose car is that?
I don't know

Are you Lost?
I don't know

Did the mail come?
I don't know

Who's that?
I don't know

So,

If you don't know
Any of this shit
Why are we talking about it?

I don't know?

Have you lost your $#&*%#$ mind?
I don't know

Who wrote this $#&*%#$ poem anyway?
I don't know.

It kinda sucks, Right?

You got that Right.

8/3/2020 #80

Day 46 "It Took all Day"

The clouds were dark when I rose
They became darker with the passing hours
It began to rain, thunder and hail
No rainbows over pristine hills
No meadows of blooming flowers

Just I, alone in a deep dark haze
A haze that would not pen
The thoughts within.

It was then that I went
To my garden gate
And there within, a host
Of little creatures were
Fluttering about.

The fun they were having
Was brilliantly insane
They had no cares
No faulty airs
Just joys as they flittered and fluttered about

The sky opened wide
The dark haze vanished
My brain changed to a brilliant blue
I began to smile.

As these fluttering stars
Once again lit the path to
The joy of a simple life
I began to laugh and skip about

8/4/2020 #80

Day-46 Red Wine Tales "Spilling Red Wine"

I always wear white

When dinking red wine

She thinks I shouldn't

But I say what the heck

A least she will know

What I've been doing

                                                              8/4/2020 #81

Day-46 "Pesky Little Pest"

Running around the
Rim of my glass
A pesky little creature stalked.
First his toe tested the heat
Then his snout took a sip
Then he jumped right in
And there he floated for most of an hour
Paddling and stroking, flipping and flopping
Round and round as if he were the
Happiest little creature in the world

Can you imagine what that little feller
Thought when he saw my big white teeth
And my lips on the rim of that glass
Ready to devour him with just one gulp?

It is my solemn belief that you
Treat all creatures with equal respect.
So, I decided to give him a reprieve
I just took a sip
And then another and another
Until there was but a puddle left

As he squirmed and twisted
In what remained I decided it was time
To release this pesky little pest
From this tiny puddle of wine

I could have smacked him with my hand
Or just tossed him to the wind
However, I decided to spill
Him on the tabletop
To see what he would do.

Once free of the puddle
And much to my astonishment
He rose and staggered about.
And off the table, he stumbled.

Drunk little bastard
He had been so much fun to watch
I hope he can find his way home
Or another lass with a glass
Of Cabernet Sauvignon

8/4/2020 #82

Have you ever noticed that red wine attracts tiny little fruit flies? I have always wondered if they get drunk. They must, for it seem to be quite the aphrodisiac.

Day-47 "Aphrodisiac"

Tis garnish for the love in your soul
It cascades through your brain
Delighting the mind

Oh, Sweet Aphrodite, come hither
Sprinkle euphoria on our paths
Rain joy and mirth from the heavens above
Shower the earth with rainbows and daisies
Sing to us in the evening hours
Teach us to dance to a thousand harps

Oh, Goddess of Love
Garnish our souls with glee and hilarity
Plant seeds of beauty in our pristine meadows
Remind us to pleasure others more than ourselves
For the gifting of "JOY" is the greatest aphrodisiac of all

8/5/2020 #83

Day-48 "Saying Goodbye"

I lost a friend today
A stark reminder how
Time takes us all

I've promised not to be sad
But to remember all those
Who have passed through my life
As the gifts they truly have been to my own.
I will honor and cherish them
Till time takes my own.

So, thank you my dear friend
For sharing with me your life
Without you I would be nothing
But dust on an empty slate

Let me toast you with a smile
You have blessed me with
Many a fond memory

8/6/2020 #84

Yesterday five acquaintances left this earthly life. It is not that they were great lifelong friends of mine. They were people I have known over the course of my life. It does indeed make me sad, and I am sure it makes you sad whenever someone departs us for another world. The key is to remember the times they brought "Joy" to your life and for you to celebrate that joy. It does and will bring peace to your soul.

Day-48 "Flowers for My Love"

I went to my garden plot

Picked flowers for my love

Roses, Violets and Daisies

Yellows, reds, and blues

A purple here and there

I placed them in a golden vase

Tied a ribbon around its pristine neck

Left it there for her to find

When she awakes and finds me gone

Their fragrance will remind

The love we shared that summer's eve.

8/6/2020 #85

Day-49 "Spice for My Soul"

Their tantalizing aroma
Drew me near
Delighting my pores

For fun, I stole a few
Placed them in my hand
And squeezed them tight

Their sensual fragrance
Bathed my spirit
Ravished my brain

This handful of lavender
A bouquet for my soul
Journeyed with me all the day

Was Spice to My Soul

8/7/2020 #86

Go to your garden and pick a handful of flowers. Put them in your hand and squeeze the fragrance out of them. Let the scent settle on your skin. Is an aphrodisiac for your soul.

Day-49 "Let it Rain"

There is "Joy" in my heart today
It rained "Joy" this morning

As I gazed across the meadows of my mind
I decided it was a great day for rain
The kind of rain that blesses your soul
Cleanses your mind
Makes you kind
I call it a "Joyous" rain

Let it rain, Let it rain
Rain melodies and harmonies
Rain happiness and prettiness

Rain snowcapped mountain peaks
Rain tall, masted ships on ocean's blue
Let it rain, Let it rain

Rain flowers for hours
Rain stars from galaxies far
Let it rain, Let it rain

Rain peace and tranquility
Rain justice and respectability
Let it rain, Let it rain

Rain laughter and goodness
Rain kindness and Joy
Rain faith, hope and charity
Let it rain, Let it rain

Let it rain my "Joyous Rain"

8/7/2020 #87

Day-50 "You Made My Day"

I read a poem today"
It made my day
This is what I am talking about
Building bridges
Looking for the good
Looking for the happy
Looking for the spice in your life
Yes, Yes, Yes.

So many years ago
A poet writes.
The way I feel
The way we need to feel.
Frances Ellen Watkins Harper
"You made my day"
I honor your prose
I read it many times
                        8/8/2020 #88

Find time to read this poem by Frances Ellen Watkins Harper

Day-50 "You Never Know"

You never know
What may come your way
Life a surprise
Each and every day

Be it on a walk about a park
An early morning read
A news cast or a show
A newborn in a crib
So many things may come your way

Sit still and listen
A bird is chirping
A stream is flowing
A soft breeze is blowing
A soft voice is speaking
Someone says, I love you
So many things may come your way

The way you see it
The way you hear it
The way you breathe it
The heart feels it

Is "Joy" for your soul
So many things may come your way
I read a great poem today

8/8/2020 #89

Day-51 "Wonderment"

Have you ever wondered
What you could do
If you could steal a day
Keep it just for you

Have you ever wondered
What you would be
If you could change a sentence
In your book of life

Have you ever wondered
If you had never met
That girl you married
50 years ago, today

Have you ever wondered
What your life would be
Had you been born black
Instead of white

Have you ever wondered
What it's like
To be an eagle
Flying high up in the sky

Have you ever wondered
How others thought of you
If you smiled
Instead of frowned

Have you ever wondered
What your life would be
If you could change
That one bad day

Have you ever wondered
How your life would have changed
Had you stayed the course
And never walked away

Have you ever wondered
About the wonder in your life
Had you always kissed the day
With a smile

I wonder all the time
But am more happy
When I don't
      For
This is where I am

Just find the wonder in you wonder
The smile in your smile
The happy in your happy
The charity in your charity
The good in your good
      And
The Love in your Love

                                          8/9/2020 #90

Day-52 "Fantastic Words"

I wrote ten fantastic words
Called them words from happy
For they were beautiful
They were alluring and exciting
Charming and delighting
Amazing and adoring
Dashing and daring

I put them in my pocket
And whenever the clouds are gray
I pull one out and speak it twenty times.
I dare you to do the same

                                                8/10/2020 #91

Day-52 "Practice Perfects"

He who practices good words
Will have good thoughts

She who sings praises
Will lead a noble life

You cannot win at Joy
Unless you embed
Beautiful words and praises
In your soul

Practice perfects the soul
The more you practice
The more brilliant your soul

                                                8/10/2020 #92

Day-52 "Liquid Diets"

Red, red wine
Makes you feel fine

Ice cold beer
You have no fear

Whisky shots
Hit the spot

Marij-hoochie
Makes you goosey

Pass the cookies please

                                                                8/10/2020 #93

Day-54 "Can I Borrow a Smile"

It gets in the way
Ruins your day
It is the opposite of love

Can you tell me what it is
Why it does this to me
Why I stomp and stammer
I need to know
It's forever in my way

Can I share one of your smiles?
Would you be so kind?
I could use one now

I promise to give it back
That was my last
Bottle of wine

                                                                  8/12/2020 #94

I was touchy, high octane mad. The challenge was how to turn a bad day into something light and gay. I'm much happier now.

Day-54 "Screw it"

Turn up the heat
Beat those drums
Blow that sax
Fire those engines
Do some high-octane shouting
Pour gas on your tongue
Spit fire from your brain
Dance across those flames
If that doesn't work
Just go pee in the rain.

                                                                  8/12/2020 #95

Day-55 "The Little Things"

How little things
Can change your life
Cleanse the rivers in your mind

How little things
Can make you happy
Make you jump for joy
Go skipping down the street

How little things
Can dress you in happiness
A flower from a friend
A peck on your cheek

How little things
Mean a lot
A poem told in the dark
A note from your lover

How little things
Can spring oceans of tears
When said just right
A Thank You for the night

How little things
Are like sweet tea
On a summer's day
      Or
Hot chocolate
On a winters eve

How little things
Are a stroll in the park
      Or an
Old couple holding hands
Cherishing their lasting hours

How little things
Are but tiny sparks
That have lit many a fire
In the annals of time

                                              8/13/2020 #96

Day-56 "Landscapes"

"Landscapes" El Capitan, Yosemite National Park

Rolling hills of daffodils
Cherry trees in springtime bloom
Fields of Kansas wheat
Aspen trees in autumn hue
Snowcapped mountain peaks

Giraffes on African plain
Mountain goats on rocky ledge
Wild horses running free
Coyotes howling at the moon

Wedding carriage in Central Park
Picnic on seaside shore
Setting sun in Michigan
Basketball on concrete lots

Paintings of our world
Hang on walls in museum halls
Captured by men and women
With steady hands and
Sharing hearts

To them we thank
The beauty of their gifts
The magic of their strokes
Standing beside the
Rivers running through
The meadows of their minds

8/14/2020 #97

Day-56 "Pheromones"

Those tiny little things
That soar from your pen
Reaching out to those around
Never knowing where they might land
They do it without a plan

Seduce or reduce
Rejoice or offend
Depends upon the kind
Are you funny and gay
Or grumpy and dumpy

Not enough of one
Maybe too much for another
Act or react
Mate or debate
They soar about us all the time
They are but scented words

8/14/2020 #98

Day-57 "Scented Words"

Beautiful thoughts
Come as beautiful words
From the garden in your mind

Colorful thoughts
Come on palettes
Roses, lilacs and lilies
From the garden in your mind

Sensual thoughts
Come as candles lit
Jasmine, lavender and cinnomint
From the garden in your mind

Joyful thoughts
Come in vases full
Daisies, violets and tulips
From the garden in your mind

Bouquets of scented words
From the beauty of your garden mind
Beguiles my senses.
I lust the lavender of your thoughts

8/15/2020 #99

Day-58 "Smilestones"

100 was a challenge
But I did it

Some said I couldn't
But I did it

Some said I wouldn't
But I did it

Some were good
But I did it

Some were bad
But I did it

Did I build a bridge?
Some said I did

Some said I didn't

Did I make you laugh?
Some said I did

Some said I didn't

Did I find Joy?
Did you?

Did the sky part
And the sunshine through?

Did a lightning bolt
Bite you in the ass,
Wake you from
Your dreary thoughts?
I hope it did   8/15/2020 #100

Day-59 "A Journey is a Journey'

A journey is a Journey
Full of this's and that's
Shoulda's and coulda's and woulda's

Sometimes you're
Stuck in the mud
A dark cloud over
Your head
Or
Sitting on a pot of gold
A rainbow in your
Rear view mirror

It can rain tears
Or bring many smiles
Lots of miles to go
A surprise at every turn

A journey is a Journey

Oh, What the Hell
Let's give it another try
365 or Bust

Saddle up folks
Buckle those spurs
This old horse ain't done yet.

Let's go find those smilestones
A journey is a Journey

8/16/2020 #101

Day-59 "Yeas and Nays"

The world is full of
Yeas and Nays

If you forever
Look for Nays

You'll never
Find the Yeas.

                                                          8/16/2020 #102

Day-59 "Spare Me"

I don't need to know
All your problems

Just your good ones
Will be fine

                                                          8/16/2020 #103

Day-60 "My Notebook"

A sentry by my side
Ready for the fight
Even in the night
Saber always drawn

A treasure trove
Of unwritten verse
Paints not mixed
Loves not found
Unfinished dreams
Melting pot of wishful thoughts

Quick the kettle calls
The steam is billowing high
Harness it before the fire dies

Raise high the saber
Put it to the test
Fill the pages
With your lust.
Put a joy on every line

My faithful companion
Never wanders
Always by my side

8/17/2020 #104

Day-60: "The End"

A phenomenon beyond description
A mystic aura enveloped the scene
Pretty girls began to dance
And kiss the boys
In their beloved towns

The streets were filled with joy
There was music
In the band shell once again

Stardust fell from
The star filled night
The moon reached out
And touched the sky

The jester shed his tears
And began to sing
The church bells
Bellowed out their rings

We danced in the street
Till the sun rose
Over the eastern plains
The war had found its end

8/17/2020 #105

It was Seventy-five years ago on August 15, 1945, when Japan surrendered marking the end of WWII.

Day-60 "Mysterious"

You know what it is
But it can't be seen
It hovers all around
A golden mist surrounds

Mysterious is its claim
That few can truly own
I said she had it then
I say she has it now

So lovely is the thought
That she and I have lain
Joy was her name
In my heart she lies
An aura that pleasures all
My inner sighs

8/17/2020 #106

Day-61 "Feel the Words"

When you say them
Can you feel them?

When you sing them
Can you hear them?

When you read them
Can you feel them?

When you see them
Can you believe them?

When you touch them
Do you love them?

When you smell one
Do you taste it?

When you see Happy
Do you smile?
Do you feel ecstatic?

When you see Alluring
Does it grab you?
Does it draw you in?

When you see Fantastic
Do your eyes light up?
Are you amazed?
When you see Amorous
Do you feel softness?
A lover's touch?

When you see Brilliant
Is it a shining star
Or an Amazing feat?

When you see Adventure
Do you get excited
Eager for the thrill?

When you shout Amazing
Does your brain come alive?
Do flip flops when it rains?

When you see one
Does it come alive?
Does it jump right off the page?
Does it run around in your brain
Or take you for a ride on a mystic cloud?

They all have reasons
They all have seasons
They are but treasures
For your pleasure

Just pick one
Any lovely one will do
Plant a vision in your brain
Let the image grow
Effervescence in your soul
Can you feel it now?

8/19/2020 #107

Day-61 "Giving Life"

They come alive
Whenever you

See them

Speak them

Read them

Write them

Smell them

Touch them

They are both

Rich and Poor

Bright and dull

Brilliant and Soft

Funny and Sad

Happy and Glad

They all have

A Reason and a Season

Only you can

Give them life.

"Words"

8/19/2020 #108

Day-61: "They Are"

They are who we are
They define us all
How we use
How we play
How we dream
How we give
How we live

The meanings we are
The games we play
The errors we make
The joys we have
The judgments we yield

They are who I am
They are who you are
They determine
As only words can

"Words"

8/19/2020 #109

Day-61 "They are choices"

They are
Verses, Scripts and Songs

They are
Love, Life and Looks

They are
Black, Brown and White

They are
Attitudes, Platitudes and Gratitudes

They are
All things Good
If we so choose

"Words" 8/19/2020 #110

Day-62 "Love Songs"

I'm sure they're love songs
Two chirping birds
High in a tree
Singing songs
To each other
In the crisp morning air

Two meadowlarks
On fence posts
Whistling in
A prairie breeze

Doves on rooftops
Cooing
On a summer's eve

Coyotes howling
On moon lit nights

I'm sure they are love songs
Their beautiful tones
Simplistic they are
Only they understand
Their very own
I love you songs

                                        Lon 8/20/2020 #111

Day-62 "Beaming"

Have you ever
Put a smile on your face
And walked down the street

Said "Good Morning"
To all who passed
On your morning walk

Have you ever
Laughed out loud
At a table for two
On Fifth Avenue

Packed a lunch
To eat on a hill

Have you ever
Borrowed a beer
From the table
Next door

Tickled the waiter
Who had a big frown

Have you ever
Told a joke with
No one around
Then laughed
At how silly it was

Have you ever
Kissed a cop
With a baton
After she
Broke it over your head

Have you ever
Borrowed a cab
To take a short ride
Then found out
You hadn't a dime

Have you ever
Told a joke
That wasn't a joke
And everyone laughed
But you

Have you ever
Told a Priest a fib
That wasn't a lie
And wondered why
He fell out of his chair
And started to cry

It's called "Beaming"
You should give it a try
No need to wonder why
It just seems to work

8/20/2020 #112

Day-63 "49 Years"

Remember that day
That bright sunshiny day
That day we gathered
And spoke our vows

On a whim we decided
To give it a try
And here we are today
Bringing back that day
Full of dreams
Nothing to our name
Yet here we are
Still picking flowers
Still taking walks
Still taking life in
Still full of dreams

Dreams of a different sort
Places to be seen
Moments with loved ones

Sitting quietly on the porch
A glass of red
Watching the sunset over the plain

Unfolding journeys
Yet to behold
Watching them grow
Round and round they go
Many miles of play
Many miles yet to go

We'll dress ourselves in smiles
And kiss each day
As it comes our way.
Many miles yet to go

                                                8/21/2020 #113

To My Wife With Love

Day-63 "Done In"

I met Margarita today
She took me for a ride
Then I met her sister
Her name was Margarita too
Before they were done
They had me on the floor
I guess I'm not as good as I used to be
On the rocks, no salt please

                                                8/21/2020 #114

Day-64 "Sharing"

Come, Share a day with me
Come, walk a mile with me
Come, share a smile with me
Come, share a laugh with me
Come, write a song with me
Come, share your time with me
Come, sit by me and
We'll sing songs all night long

Come, share a moment
Even when it rains
The sun will surely shine

                                                8/22/2020 #115

Day-66 "Caring"

How far did you say it was?
To where we are going

I didn't
I said it can be as close as you want
Or as far as can be

So where are we are going?

"Caring"
I said we are going to "Caring"

"Caring" what?

Where is this place called "Caring"?
Is it a town?
Is it a country?
I didn't know there was a place called "Caring"

Well, there is
Sometimes it is here
And sometimes it is there
And sometimes right in front of you

That doesn't make any sense
If it was here and there
And in front of me
I could see it.
If I cannot see it, it doesn't exist.

Oh, my friend
I can tell
You have not traveled far
Take my hand and follow me
For there are many people, places and things
Abiding in "Caring"

Look... Look over there

See that stream
Running through the vale
See how clear it is
See the beautiful trout

See the old man
With a cane
Little boy by his side
School bus up ahead

See the man in blue
A pouch of letters
From friends far away
Thinking of you
Happy birthdays too

See those children in the park
One falls off
Another picks him up

There's a couple on a bench
Sharing lunch
Sharing lives

See the man
Pick up that cup
Left by someone else

Watch the boy
Who opens the door
Letting the lady pass

See the nurse
Holding that poor man's hand

See the man on the corner
Could use a quarter in his cup
Let's fill it up

There's a lady
Tending her garden
Flowers blooming

Can you see it yet?

I think I can
Tell me more

This place I call caring
Is in your heart
It's in your spirit
It's a state of mind

It's your love of all things
Great and small
Your love of all mankind

It's how you live
Of what you take
Of what you need

It's caring about
Those you may not know
Caring about your friends
Caring about the little ones in this world.

It's like sending a card
Or lending a hand
Cleaning the stream that flows
Lifting a spirit that's down

When trouble comes
You share your gifts
It's a state of mind
Do you see it now?

Yes, Yes
I think I could live here

8/24/2020 #116

"The Power of Color"

It occurred to me that something was changing inside my mind as I traveled down this happiness journey. That I was feeling happier, more robust, more free than ever before. What was it I asked myself? Was it just the fact that I was saying good morning to my family, recognizing all the travels and places we have been or the shouting out of the music I have been listening to? It wasn't just the smiles or the beautiful scenery and memories on my walls. There was something more to it. There was something else bringing Joy to my life. As perplexed as I was it dawned on me that color was playing a major role in this happiness journey. The reds, greens, blues, oranges and pinks on my walls were interacting with my brain in unseen ways. Underneath all the blankets of my life I was discovering the enlightening and beautiful colors hidden there. I discovered that I really needed color in my life and that my life wasn't defined just by a beautiful, loving face or place on my wall. That my words were being enhanced by the colors they exemplified. That words are colors as well as colors are words. That the two mix and mingle in unseen ways bringing joy and happiness to life. They need each other just as people need each other. They both paint pictures of your life.

Enough said. I decided I needed to look at the meaning of colors and how they affect people and the roles they play in defining your inner being. As presented below, I am defining the underlying meaning of what the colors imply in the following ten poems, as I understand them. I have also discovered the significance of the selection of colors and their shades used by artists in their respective mediums. It has been an interesting journey. So here goes and I hope you sincerely enjoy.

Day-65 "Color it Purple"

Opening this door
Should not surprise
What lies inside
For those who
Summarize

It's full of sights unseen
Bright lights and mysterious scenes
That come and go
As the tumbler turns

Pick a rose
And let it grow
Flush the haze
From your gaze

Pick another
Let your juices flow
The many places
It will glow

The challenge
Is to find the one
That fits you best
It is but
The color of your brain.
That lets you live in harmony

It enlightens your soul
And makes you whole
Let's you love without fear
Mines your hidden gold

Reigns over the power within
Allows the life you live

Creates the space you own
Makes it solely yours alone

Is but the color you paint today
Yours to choose
"Purple" is its name

                                          8/26/2020 #117

Day-65 "Color it Black"

It's a negligee
That teases with the brain
Is power and lust
Much the same

It's fiery, frisky and feisty
It's dark silken hair
Flaming desire
On satin sheets

It's a cup of java
Without cream
Prepares the day
That has no dream

Its seductive aroma
Pleases the flavor
Arouses the flower
That grows within

It's the heat
On a summer's eve
A starless night
When you're all alone

It's a silk tie
A little black dress
Cocktails for two
Seductive delights

Undeniably true
Powerful its hue
Captivating too
When paired with
A Smile

Color it "Black"
As Black can be so
Powerfully sexy

                                  8/26/2020 #118

Day-65 "Color it Pink"

It's deliciously enticing
Alluringly inviting
Delightfully divine

It grows on rosy cheeks
Clings to popsicle sticks

Full of romance
In front of a fire
On a snowy eve

It is invitingly insane
It draws love
From an artist's palette

Infectiously kind
Fills the heart and soul
With compassion and love

Calms the heart
In the heat of the day

Puts lipstick on your soul.
A twinkle in your eye

Is hopelessly romantic
"I love you hearts"
On "Valentine's Day"

Can be flirtatiously frisky
At a table for two
And a bottle of red

It is but the universal
Color of Love.

Call it "Pink"
My most favorite one

8/26/2020 #119

Day-66 "Color it Green"

Relaxing the scene
The meadow green
Karma supreme

Bath in its lushness
Tumble in its coolness
Relish in its freshness

Open your eyes
To her generosity
Your lover to be
Nature your Amour

She will not deny
The trail
Through the forest
Of your mind

She brings comfort
With open arms
Your head seized
By your heart

Oceans to swim
Mountains to climb
Alive in your mind
Pleasures divine

Renew your vows
In meadows lush
The forests flush
With pots of gold
At rainbow's end

Her glorious gifts
Grow "Spring" in the
Shadows of your life
Karma for your soul

She Colors you **"Green"**

8/26/2020 #120

Day-66 "Color it Blue"

A real jewel
This color blue
It's really cool

It's your trusted
Best friend

Your Bliss
When you're amiss

Peace and tranquility
Its middle name

Uplifts your spirit
Paints your sky
In multiple shades

Asks nothing of you
Teller of truth
Giver of gifts

Leads you to
An ocean shore
Serenading waves
Sand in your toes

Look up at the sky
A beautiful hue
Lie on your back
And enjoy the view

A real jewel
This color "Blue"

8/27/2020 #121

Day-67 "Color it Yellow"

It's a beautiful hue
The early morning sun
Rising over the plains
Kissing the sunflowers
As they reach for its rays
Children, laughing and chatting
Leaving for school
Greetings from a lady
As they scurry aboard

An artist, brushing and stroking
A taxicab scene
Bringing life to a canvas
So, we may see

A ribbon tied to a tree
A mother awaiting
Her husband to be

Others not like me
Dancing in the street
Taking my hand
Singing gospel songs
To a haloed man

A man in his submarine
Sailing around the world
To catch a sunset
Just before dawn

A polka dot bikini
On a beach of sand
A treasure to enjoy
If it ever gets lost

Oh, what a fun way to live
When given a chance
Because it's so mellow
Color it "**Yellow**"   8/28/2020 #122

Day-67 Color it Brown

You've been mother of being
For millions of years
Your skin tinted
Shades of clay

Full of wisdom and knowledge
History and lore
Her mouth explodes
When she finds us wrong

From her bowels
Come fruits and roots
Her harvest bountiful
When we smile
And do things right

She brings joy to the valley
When rivers run fresh
With peace and harmony

A peaceful solitude
Reigns in her court
That the winds of time
Cannot erode

The peace that comes
When truth becomes true
Unveils the beauty
Of heavenly souls

Dear Mother Earth
I crown you "Brown"

8/28/2020 #123

Day-69 "Color it White"

So many symbols
This color enjoys

So many emotions
This color evokes

Angelic Angels and
Jesus Christ
Purity personified

Wedding vows and
Wedding veils

Innocent child
Untainted lives

White hats on
Stallions bold

Cherry blossoms
Welcoming the spring

Sparkling clean
Fit for a queen

Damsels in need
Little girl dreams

Stars in the sky
Galaxies far away

Sails on the sea
Chasing a breeze

Cotton ball clouds
Sailing the blue
Soft falling snow
Stars on Christmas trees glow

Color it "White"   8/30/2020 #124

Day-69 "Color it Orange"

It stands alone
On rocky hills

Embraces many a
Morn on seaside shores

Blazing skies
In evening rays

Power its fame
Brilliance its game

Very few have
Conquered its fire

Left alone it
Fuels desire

Spontaneous combustion
Its only friend

The artist paints
It with a glow in his eye
A nail in his soul.
A message to behold.

Paint your sky
With this color
It will make you bold

Color it "Orange"

8/30/2020 #125

Day-71 "Color it Red"

The hottest color
Of them all
Burning embers
In an artist's eye

Passion its game
Desire its claim
Lovers beware the
Fire it flames

It claims your heart
Enslaves your soul
Melts resistance
To its core
It makes you jump
Cry out in joy
Shakes the rafters
In your mind

Yours to own
But for a while
Take it in
With a smile

It's bold and strong
Take it now
Before it's gone

Light the candles
Share some red
Whisper love words in her ear
Take her home to bed
Let the flames burn hot and red

Color it "**Red**"   8/30/2020 #126

Day-72 "Treasures"

A friend gave it to me one day
A tiny little box
He said to keep it
And hide it far away
Where no one will ever find
Yours to open
On melancholy days

I found a little stone
And placed it in that box
And hid it far away
Was the day we strolled?
Along that sandy beach

You wrote a little note
I placed it in that box
And hid it far away
Was a secret
That we shared
No one else will ever know

She gave a lock
Of hair and
Tied it with a yellow bow
I placed it in that box
And hid it far away

She gave a key
One eve
To open up her door
I placed it in that box
And hid it far away

I remember well
The kiss she left
On the napkin where
We dined
I placed it in that box
And hid it far away

Tiny photos
Of my loves
I placed them in that box
And hid it far away
To pull it out
When I'm lonely
Old and tinted gray

They put a smile
On my face
And warm this old cold heart
For they are treasures of my time
And memories of my prime

Some day
Someone will find
My little box
And wonder what these meant
To the man who left
Them here
And why he never
Let them go

9/1/2020 #127

Day-73 "Donna My Love"

You are the sunshine
In my day

You are the Joy
In my heart

You are the Love
Of my life

You are the keeper
Of my soul
The one who makes me whole

If I were never to write another
You would be the last I'd write

For you are my poem
The poetry in my life

                                            9/2/2020 #128

Today is Donna's birthday.

Day-74 "Surprises"

Around every corner
Lies something never seen

Beyond every hill
An untouched vale

Behind closed doors
An untold story

Beneath a blanket
Heavenly dreams

Open the door
Someone you've known
From long ago

A box and a bow
On your front step
Who's it from
You would like to know

Don't tell me what
Don't tell me where
Just pick me up at 10:00 PM

A blind date
Please come and
Whisk me away
Where did you say
The restroom lay

Answer the damn phone
Who it this you say?
Oh my God!
You're standing outside

They make you laugh and
Jump with joy
Lose your breath
And faint on the floor

Yes... many break hearts
When they part
Yet many bring joy
When they "Surprise"
You with a rose.

9/2/2020 #129

Day-74 "Surprises-2"

The words that come out
How we organize and contemplate
How we pick and choose
The end is never known
Creates quite a thrill
When we are through
"Surprises" even me

9/2/2020 #130

Day-76 "Crossing Over"

You have to cross over
Leave your doubts and fears behind
It's not an easy task
Come...
You have to cross over

The river is full
Of rocks and rapids
Of slips and spills
And trembling trills
But it won't kill
You have to cross over

What awaits
The other side
Can never be known
Throw caution aside
One step at a time
You have to cross over

A life without joy
Is a boy without a toy

A life without lust
Is full of distrust

A life without compassion
Has no passion

You have to trust for it
Will make you complete
You have to cross over

One step at a time
Put a smile on your face
Your fate is yours to decide

One step at a time
Put a little joy in your heart
The river isn't that wide

You'll see in a while
Putting love in your soul
The difference it makes
One step at a time

You'll learn to fly
Over valleys of despair
Soaring high with the eagles
One step at a time

When two trails cross
You'll know which to take
To the crystal-clear lake
Where happiness reigns

But you'll never know
Unless you cross over
Come.... Take my hand
And cross over with me.

                                          9/4/2020 #131

Day-77 "Rhythms"

Rock and Roll
Round and round
The 45's go

Ocean waves
To and fro
Kissing the sandy shore

Listen to your heart
It has a beat
Often fast
Sometimes slow

Back and forth
The old swing sways
Little girl squeals
Daddy's delight

Pendulums swing
Metronomes click
Jump ropes twirl
One misstep
Throws you amiss

She blossoms in the spring,
Matures in the summer
Harvests her bounty
In the fall and
Wraps herself in blankets
When winter calls

Some call it a beat
Some call it a dance
Some call it a song
Some call it a rhyme
Some call it a pattern

To some it's sameness
To some it's saneness
To many it is a life
They cannot live without

9/5/2020 #132

Day-77 "Your Smiling Face"

"Your Smiling face"

Plants flowers

In

My heart

"Your Smiling Face"

Brings

Sunshine

To

My autumn

"Your Smiling Face"

I Love

9/5/2020 #133

Day-78 "Haikus"

"Nature's Moments"

Crispy mountain air
Rocky trails pass trout filled streams
Early morning hike

Early morning suns
Orangish paint through seashore pier
Beauty knows not time
Setting summer suns
Orange paint over mountain pass
Beauty knows not time

Western Kansas winds
Meadowlarks sing prairie songs
Whisper ancient lives

Painted deserts rise
Far beyond what eyes can see
History knows not peace

Painted scarlet red
Mother Earth is crying out
Flames are burning fast

9/6/2020 #134

Day-78 "Two trails"

Two trails cross
You have to choose
Which one to take
Always a choice
Not an easy task
When you're just
Out for an evening stroll

9/6/2020 #135

Day-78 "A Boot in the Ass"

You've come to a crossroad
You have to make a choice
Which one will you choose?
You've lingered too long

I know, I know
I'm through
I'm through cussing and discussing
I'm through contemplating and meditating
I'm through doubting and pouting

I'm through, I'm through

I'll just take that one over there

      "Now"

Would you mind pulling your
Boot out of my ass.

                                        9/4/2020 #136

The moral of this poem is; sometimes you need a little prodding.

Day-79 "Equine Rhythms"

I walked my stead today
Over rocks and grassy plains
I wanted a leisurely ride

It's faster than a walk
It's spicy and tart
It is the trot

A galloping horse
Is ridden hard and fast
You must be in a hurry
To ride a horse this way

Its rhythm intoxicating
Two bodies rising and flowing
True beauty in symphonic motion
Man and horse as one
My most favorite ride
The Lope

9/7/2020 #137

Day-79 "Adventure"

Every day is one
Every day becomes one
They excite the soul
Burn flames in your brain

No matter where you are
No matter who you are
No matter the treasure you have
There is one to seek
Even when they're meek

They hide behind doors
In gardens galore
Sunsets on ocean shores

Poets spinning rhymes
Blind men counting dimes

Far too many
For me to chime
The excitement that awaits
When there's a smile
Upon your face
A gleam in your eye
And a skip in your gait
An adventure every day

9/7/2020 #138

Day-80 "What the Hell"

What are we to do today?
This cold came bursting in
It's much too early for snow
The leaves have yet to fall
I'm wondering if we have sinned
We'll play some cards
And drink some gin
Lay on a bear skin rug
In front of a fire
That has no fire

We'll go outside
Turn cartwheels in the snow
Throw snowballs at the sun
Scamper off to heaven
Somewhere south of here

We'll curse the crew
Who brought it here
Trade them in for snowshoes
And hearty glasses of beer

It's only September eight
And I have yet to find a mate
That likes bear skinned rugs
And fires that have no fire

Me thinks I'll
Take my bony limbs outside
And wait for June to come again.

If she ever will

I once knew a girl named June
I think it's her
Still mad as hell   9/8/2020 #139

Day-80 "Kiss Me"

Purple is the color of
My true love's hair
She tied it in a knot
And bound it with a yellow bow
Said kiss me if you want

Orange is the color of
My true love's nails
She put a diamond on each one
Said kiss me if you want

Green is the color of
My true love's eyes
She grew her lashes long
Penciled in her brows
Much to my surprise
Said kiss me if you want

Gold is the color
Of that thing stuck in her tongue
She put it there forever
Never to come out
Said kiss me if you want

Black is the color
Of an eagle on her back
She bought it in Saint Louie
From a man named Tim Dewey
Said kiss it if you want

So naïve am I
That I kissed her everywhere
And still dream of eagle feathers
Way down there.

9/8/2020 #140

Day-81 "Last of the Haikus"

Ladies in red hats
Sitting in a garden spot
Drinking cups of tea

Little boys and girls
Counting numbers one two three
Playing hide and seek

Monday morning blues
Snow has fallen on the porch
Let's stay home and play

Magpie in a tree
Tweeting loud his morning chirp
Driving all insane

Laughter in the air
Wind blows through her lovely hair
Tattoo on her thigh

Joyful is the prose
Grumpy faces turned to dust
Grows smiles on the face

Written on a pad
Three hundred and sixty-five
Days of joyful prose

Brilliant not this prose
Hallelujahs all around
Haikus finally done   9/9/2020 #141

I've discovered that making Haikus funny is most difficult; they are more exercises in technique, something you need to try every once in a while. I promise not to do any more. I'll just leave them for some Chinese guy.

Day-81 "Gladly Meets Happy"

Red door up the stairs
Tiny knob made of gold
A sign read
Come in with a smile
And stay with us awhile

Thereupon I pushed the knob
It opened just a crack
The doorman asked;
Do you have a smile upon your face?
No frowns allowed you know
I think I do,
Can you tell me if I do?

I believe you do but
You need to tweak it just a bit
Then I'll let you through

Whereupon I spun around
And pushed my jaws way up high
And puckered up my lips
And kissed the doorman on the cheek

He jumped up high and
Clicked his heels
And opened wide the door
And told me with a smile
You're the kind we like the best

People everywhere
Jumping up and down
Twirling round and round
On the tables, down the halls
Holy Molies everywhere
Laughter bouncing off the walls
It was a "dazzling" affair

A little lady grabbed my arm
And flung me way up high
So high I wondered if I could fly
But she caught me when I fell
And spun me round the room
Introducing me to all
Said I was from Mars.
And was a rising star

I asked her name
She replied with a smile
As wide as a mile

Said she was Happy
Happy go here and
Happy go there
Happy go everywhere
Happy go crazy
Happy go lucky
If you don't care.

And yours? She asked

My name is Gladly
Gladly I'm here
Gladly I'm not there
Gladly to go crazy
With someone like you

Whereupon I spun around
And pushed my jaws way up high
And puckered up my lips
And kissed Happy on her cheek
Whereupon Happy opened up her doors
And gladly let me in

We make quite a pair don't you think?
Crazy as it sounds
Insane it really is
Aren't you glad we're Gladly Happy now?
9/9/2020 #142

Day-82 "Free"

Free, Free, Free
I want to be Free
Free to be me
Free to laugh
Free to write
Free to speak
That's what I want
Freedom to be Free

9/10/2020 #143

Day-82 "Free to be"

Did you ever think
You could be Free
Free to Be
Free to Do
Free to Go
Free to Leave
Free to Love
Free to Hate
Free to Cry
Free to be whom you want to be?

9/10/2020 #144

Day-82 "Mind and Body"

Is your mind free?
Free to think
Free to dream
Free to choose
Free to fly in midnight skies

Is your body free?
Free to love
Free to give
Free to share
Free of sin
Free to fly in midnight skies

9/10/2020 #145

Day-82 "The Price you Pay"

To be free
There must be a fee
It can't be free

Of course, it's not free to be free
The price you pay
Is neither in gold nor script

The price you pay
Comes from your heart and soul
In the words you speak
The actions you take
The commandments you live by

Lust and Envy
Gluttony and Greed
Pride and Sloth
And, of course, Wrath
You give these up to be free
They are the price you pay
For they are but pawns residing
In the depths of your mind

It's not a high price to pay
They have no monetary value
They have no redeeming value

Once you have cashed these in
You can be free to roam,
Free to be
Free to love
Free to be content
Free to bring joy to this world.
Free to have a happy soul
Free to share your frees
Across the face of time *9/10/2020 #146*

Day-83 "Rhythm of Words"

How do you sing?
Happy, Harmony and Happily
Joy, Joyful, and Jubilee

You sing them with a smile and twinkly in your eyes

How do you say?
Love, Loved and Lovely
Passion, Pleasure and Pleasing

You say them as a message from your heart

How do you write?
Beauty, Beautiful and Beautify
Bright, Beaming, and Brilliant

You write them with a pen that knows no end

How do you define?
Exciting, Engaging and Elation
Eager, Exultant and Euphoric

You define them by praising the moments they shared with you

How do you describe?
Breathtaking and Breathless
Bliss and Blissfulness

You describe them in rhymes and midnight dreams

How do you spell?
Dazzling, Dashing and Daring
Dramatic, Delightful and Delirious

You spell them with Delights
Found in the dictionary of your mind
Always keep it open
There are many rhythms yet to find

9/11/2020 #147

Day-84 "Choose Not"

I choose not to
Write those words today

I choose not to
Hear those words today

I choose not to
Read those words today

I choose not to
Watch that show today

I choose not to
Sing that song today

I choose not to
Travel that road today

I choose not to
Speak those words today

I choose not to
For they harm my soul

Instead

I choose to write
Uplifting rhymes

I choose to play
Amusing songs with a Caribbean beat

I choose to read
Amusing words on cartoon pages

I choose to
Play in the park with a child

I choose to
Ride my bike through a Vermont vale

I choose to
Tell a joke to a passer by

I choose these over
All the impediments there are

My breath is much
Much more happy when-

9/12/2020 #148

Today is September 12, 2020. Yesterday was 9/11/2020, Nineteen (19) years after the twin towers came down. As if that wasn't enough our country is in the midst of a pandemic of profound portions, wildfires wreaking havoc on our western shores, hurricanes that have laid waste to our southern states, Black lives dying in the streets, marchers trying to reconcile as their cities burn, and our president refusing to tell the truth. Those are the words I'm talking about that I cannot write. Even though they are torching my soul I choose not to for they would defeat the purpose of these poems. My poems are written to overcome all the bleakness and depression that shrouds our lives in these most difficult times. I choose to keep it that way as I continue to bridge that river of despair.

Day 84 "Unusual Words"

Mucho Dumasso

Bet you don't know
What those words mean

But I do

They've been on this page for several weeks
Searching for a home
Perhaps even a hole to hole up in

They've been in my mind for most of my life
There usually saved for me
Especially when I have
Done something really dumb
Like, write this stupid verse.
Thank God they finally found a home.

9/12/2020 #149

Day-85 "Mix it up"

How do you feel?
Do you have a beat
That you can repeat
It would be really neat
One that would make you complete

Do you feel happy?
How about scrappy
Without being snappy

Do you feel frivolous?
In need of forgiveness
Are you superstitious?

Are you a little sensitive?
Basking in your sensuality
Being yourself discretely

If you feel the beat
Sprinkle a little happy in it
Add some frivolous
And a dash of sensuality
And your day will be complete

Have a happy day my friend

9/13/2020 #150

Day-85 "Call it Home"

Oh, you children of the sun
Gather up your stars and run
To a place that isn't far
A place without a scar

Oh, you mothers of your sons
Pick a place to have some fun

Try an ocean by a sea
A forest in the sky
A mountain that's not high

To you fathers of you daughters
Pick a place they all call home.

Fill it with love and laughter
For all their days to come

9/13/2020 #151

Day-86 "Short Song-ets of No Redeeming Value"

I want to be
As dumb as a horse
Let you ride me
Long after dusk

Pour me a glass of wine
Life is more glamorous
When you think it's not hazardous

Your kiss was tangy
Your taste was kinky
I drank it all
And a bottle of gin to boot

More wine is my desire
Till we un-attire
Merry making in the dark

I'm selling happy stars today
Two for a penny
One for you and
One for the guy I want you
To want me to be

Mesmerized I was
When you walked in
Lusty thoughts flooded my eyes
Me, thinks we
Should sin again

9/14/2020 #152

Day 87 "Nothing but Bliss"

Your blissful sighs
Are my desire
Let's rise and kiss the sun
Before the evening comes

9/15/2020 #153

Day-87 "Color Me"

Fascinating was the game
We played each night till dawn
We all were winners
Not a looser in the game
Fantastic was its name
The numbers never counted
For it never mattered
If I were it
And you were not
For we couldn't tell our colors
In the darkness of the night

9/15/2020 # 154

Day-87 "Moon Glow"

There is a smile
On his golden face
A twinkle in his eye
Something I've never
Seen before.

Maybe it's our secret
As we loved in the meadow
And gazed at the stars
That sweet summer's eve

9/15/2020 # 155

Day-88 "CAT TALES"

I wrote a flower today
And gave it to my girl
She said it was beautiful
That I should write some more
So, I wrote and wrote and wrote
But she never more did read.

I painted a song today
And gave it to a friend
He said it was beautiful
That I should paint some more
So, I painted and painted and painted
But he never came back for more

I walked a mile today
To see where it went
I walked and walked and walked
But I could not find an end
So, I turned around
And went the other way
I walked and walked and walked
Yet never found where it began.

I bought a dog
To see if he would howl
At someone knocking at my door
But all he did was snore
And pee upon my floor

I bought a cat
To see if he would chase
His tail around the room
But all he did was stare at me
Thinking I am a fool

I bought some uplifting today
To see what it would say.
It said to end this poem right now
Or I will end your day

                                          9/16/2020 # 156

Day-88 "Notebooks-2"

Notebooks are nothing more
than scribbled thoughts
thrown upon the floor.
Turn the page and you will find
I've left you many more.

                                          9/16/2020 #157

Day-91 "This Is My Day"

There is a love song
Yearning in my brain
A blue bird in my heart
Waiting to be sung

There is a poem
Living in my pen
A notebook full of rhymes
Waiting to be writ

There is beauty
In a sunrise
A day
Waiting to be lived

I'll fill it with a blue bird
Singing love songs
From my notebook
In the early dawn

                                          9/19/2020 #158

Day-91 "Redecorate"

Let's change the scenery
Remove the gloom from our halls
Put some love on the walls

Take a brush
And paint a desert wash
Full of flowers
With lots of power

Take the black of the night
Paint a little green in the light

Take the yellow from that feller
And turn him into something stellar

Take your heart
And turn it inside out

Take your soul
And turn it about

There comes a time
When we must change
Taking charge of what remains
      By
Painting happy faces on our walls

9/19/2020 #159

Day-91 "Collections"

I collect words
And store them on a shelf
In the basement of my mind

Sometimes I go there to reminisce
Sometimes I go there to find a friend
Sometimes I go there just to have some fun
Sometimes I go there just to let them out

I collect thoughts
And store them in a box
In the basement of my mind

Sometimes I go there just to hear them out
Sometimes I go there just to play with them once more
Sometimes I go there just to see if something new has come along
Sometimes I go there just to see if I have changed

I collect deeds
And store them in a bottle
In the basement of my mind

Sometimes I go there to see if they helped someone along the way
Sometimes I go there to see if I could have done something more
Sometimes I go there to see if they were good
Sometimes I go there to read of them once again

I collect memories
And store them in an album
In the basement of my mind

Sometimes I go there to see what they've become
Sometimes I go there to laugh at all the fun
Sometimes I go there to remind myself of choices in my life
Sometimes I go there just to lie with you once more
And sing those crazy songs of our younger days.

9/19/2020 #160

Wine Tales

There is nothing like a good bottle of vino and a sunny afternoon at a table for two with nothing else to do.

Day-93 "Lonely"

Sometimes I get a little confused
And feel lonely
Like a bottle of unopened wine
On a table for two
She stood me up.

9/21/2020 #161

Day-93 "Confused"

Sometimes I can't think
Of anything to say
To an empty bottle of wine
On a table for two
She forgot our date

9/21/2020 #162

Day-93 "Forgetful"

Sometimes I wonder
If I forgot to say I'm sorry
For showing up
With an empty bottle of wine
Forgetting who I shared it with

                                                  9/21/2020 #163

Day- 93 "Blew That One"

A violent storm was brewing
Inside her brain
When I showed up
With an empty bottle of wine.
I said it spilled.
She slammed the door in my face.
It was, of course, her birthday

                                                  9/21/2020 #164

Day-93 "The Prize"

I'm as Lonely as
Lonely can get
She left me for another
Taking my last
Bottle of red
For a prize

Now,

Alone I sit
I would feel much better
If she would have left me
Just a tiny sip

                                                  9/21/2020 #165

Day-93 "How to Lose Your Lover"

I spilled some on her dress
She punched me in the face
No regrets have I
For now, me thinks,
I won't have to drive her home

9/21/2020 #166

Day-93 "Share Your Happy"

I helped two ladies
With their car
I didn't ask a dime
I did it because I had the time
No need to compensate
They gave a thank you
From their hearts

We bought an item
From a five and dime
When asked how much it was
We gave it back
Said it was too much

Unbeknownst to us
The checker put it back in our sack
We asked, what for?
She paid said the checker

A lady with a smile
From ear to ear said
My gift to you.

You needn't do that
We really don't need it
We just thought it too much

Keep it she said
My gift to you
It makes me happy
Please share my happy
With someone else in need

Thank you is all we could say
So simple it seems
So gracious and kind
We will indeed
Pass it on.

Thank You So Much
Kind lady friend.

9/21/2020 #167

Day-95 "Home"

The weight so heavy
She could not bear
Welcome home my love
Welcome home

Rest your soul
Repair the hurt
Welcome home my love
Welcome home

Regain your strength
Reclaim your passion
Welcome home my love
Welcome home

Erase the time
Start anew
Welcome home my love
Welcome home

You are not lost
Reclaim your lust
Welcome home my love
Welcome home

Return with a vengeance
Only when ready
Welcome home my love
Welcome home

This place is yours
We're always here
Welcome home my love
Welcome home

When tested
We'll be here
Welcome home my love
Welcome home

                              9/23/2020 #168

For Abby, our granddaughter, as she battles COVID 19

Day-95 "Home Is"

Home is where
Little boys play ball
In back yard lots

Home is where
Little girls play mommies
Behind bedroom doors

Home is where
Daddies come home to rest
Mommies scamper little ones
Off to school

Home is where
The fragrant evening meal
Sifts through the air
Calling all to gather

Home is where
Stories are read
At bedtime hours

Home is where
You sit on a porch
In warm evening hours

Home is where
You snuggle in a blanket
Watching late night shows

Home is where
Bacon and eggs and
A glass of milk
Greet a Saturday morn

Home is where
A Christmas tree
With ribbons and bows
Decorates the room
As ancient melodies
Fill the air

Home is where
Tears are shed
When your babies marry

Home is where
You come
When you are alone

Home is where
Memories are hung
On living room walls

Home is a haven
When you are troubled
With parents who care

Home is many things
You call your own
It's where you lived
It's where you've become
Who you are.

Home is
The one you make
When you're on your own

Make it a happy one
They will come home

9/23/2020 #169

Day-96 "Waves"

What is there in a wave
That can make your day?

Is it a hand held high
As if it were a Railroad sign
        Or
Is it a hand that flutters
Like a butterfly

Does it resemble a
Military salute
        Or
A velvety touch with
A tiny little wiggle

Do you wink an eye
When you wave
        Or
Give the passer by
A great big smile

Does your wave
Show your friendly side
        Or
Your don't give a care side

Does your wave
Make you feel happy and friendly
        Or
 Dumpy and Grumpy

The ways we wave
Are choices made
In fleeting moments
To those we pass
Along our many ways

Just between you and me
Make it a happy one
It's a great way to mark your day

        9/24/2020 #170

Day-96 "Lets Go Charming"

Let's do it
Let's go charming today
I'm sure we can find
Someone along the way
Needing diamonds in their day
Don't you think that would be a lot of fun?

We could charm them with a smile
We could charm them with a kind word
We could charm them with a wink
We could charm them with a lullaby
Let's go charming today
Don't you think that would be a lot of fun?

Let's tell someone how nice they are
You are really nice!
Was so nice of you to come

Let's tell a lady how pretty she is
You are really pretty!
I love your dress

Let's tell a man he did a great job
You did a wonderful job!
We couldn't have done it without you

Let's tell her she is a fantastic painter
I love your work!
Your use of color is incredible
Let's tell your boss you like her style

I work much harder
Knowing you care

Let's tell a nurse we appreciate what she/he does
If you don't mind
I'll open the door to help you through

Let's tell the gardener he has a magical touch
Your garden is beautiful
If I only had your talent

Tell him he is handsome and strong
Tell her she is gorgeous and trim

Tell the preacher
Tell the teacher
Tell the clerk
Tell the cop

And while you are at it

The mailman
The newspaper boy
The taxicab driver
The little girls skipping rope
The little boys playing ball
The lady down the hall
The cowboy and his beautiful horse

There is nothing like a touch of charm
To brighten someone's day
I'm sure you can think of many, many more

Now, let's go out and have some fun
Spreading diamonds all around

9/24/2020 #171

Day-97 "Incredible"

Father Sun at morning light
Kisses Mother Earth
Awakens her with a smile

Rain in midnight hours
Dew drops on pastoral flowers
Sparkling in the early dawn

Fragrant breezes from the south
Carried on the wings
Of feathered friends

The moon shining bright
On snowcapped peaks
Vapor trails cross the sky

Buzzing bees
On honeysuckle leaves
Coyotes howling in the dark

Melodies of feathered friends
Lions roaring on African plains
Salmon flying up a river wall

Meadowlarks on prairie sage
Horses galloping across the plains
Arrowheads lying in the dust

Cotton ball clouds in the sky
Eagles flying high
Grand Canyon far below

Sunsets on a summer's eve
Milky Way fills the sky
Diamonds shining bright

Simple as they seem
Store them in your heart
Incredible, they really are

                        9/25/2020 #172

Day- 99 "Happy Birthday Florence"

You are such a Joy
We've known you for many years
You've known our children
And all the children on Juniper Lane
Never forgetting a name

You've watched them play and
Sometimes cry
You've watched them grow and marry
You've never forgotten a birthday
Nor an anniversary

You are the Patron Saint
Of Juniper Lane
The one we call home to
The one we keep in our prayers
The one we think of every day

Your long life
Your forgiving smile
Your Heavenly belief
Has lit many a fire
So many have you touched

Memories kept in memory books
Too many to digest in a day
Tell the story of your life
And those so touched

Your story has many acts
Played out in many scenes
From dust bowl days
To waring times
School house on prairie plain
To a rocking chair at
Florence Wilson Elementary

The little ones you've loved
With Christmas teas and
Easter egg hunts.

Wally's trees and two dollar bills
Neighborhood picnics
A name plate for everyone
We'll never forget

A grand life you've enjoyed
The way we wish to be
When we turn One Hundred too.

Happy Birthday Florence!
You are always in our thoughts
You are such a Joy

9/27/2020 #173

Written for a neighbor and lifelong friend for her 100th birthday

Day-99 "Encouragement"

It has a magical presence
Something about it
Moves mountains
Opens ocean floors
Sends tracers to the heavens

A word
Full of courage
A pat on the back
A job well done

A word that empowers
A word full of trust
A powerful word
"Encouragement"
Give it whenever you can

9/27/2020 #174

DAY-100 "TULIPS"

Photo taken in the Keukenhof Gardens

Gracing my wall
The beauty of us all
Our many colors
For all to see
For all to be

We are Yellows and Reds
Purples and Pinks
Oranges and Whites
Blacks and Browns
Together as one

We are more than colors
Of the rainbow.
We are
Beautifully divined

People of the world
Coming together
Lying together

Living together
Loving together
A collage of all
Engaging, Entrancing, Enduring
As the one
Gracing my living room wall
Tulips we are

                        9/28/2020 #175

Day-100 "Joy Spirits"

They bear the fruit of your being
They live in the misty caverns of your mind
Ghost like they thrive and multiply
On grace, love and kindness
Addictive, their sensuality

They have many names
Glorious for one
Enchanting for another

Some are Euphoric
Others are Ecstatic

Some frisky
Some feisty

They enthrall your soul
For a good deed
Embrace your smile
For a grand hello

Make you laugh
Giggle with glee
Jump up and down
On a bed made for fun

They flirt with the sky
The heavens above
The air you breathe
The water you bathe

Waiting for you
To set them free

For they are but ghosts
With many gifts
Hiding in the misty
Caverns of your mind.

        9/28/20 #176

Day-101 "Hey! Hey!"

We're off to see the mountains today.
They say there are blankets of yellow
Warming snowcapped peaks
Leaf strewn trails and
Running wild streams.
Can't wait to see.

We'll take photos
Along the way;
Grab a bite in
Quaint mountain town.
What a joy it will be
To see canyon walls
In autumn bloom,
Geese in flight and
Mountain goats
On rocky cliffs

Hey! Hey!
The sights we'll behold
We're leaving in 5.
Grab your coat
And camera too
We're off to steal the day.

9/29/2020 #177

Day-102 "Tid Bits"

I come from a land
Where never is heard
A discouraging word

That's "Bullshit"

I've said plenty and
I'm not done yet......

9/30/2020 #178

Day-102 "Tid Bits-2"

Angry words
Light fires

Happy words
Grow flowers

9/30/2020 #179

Day-102 "Tid Bits-3"

I forget too easily
Or is that forgiveness
Disguised?

"Forgetting"
Our healing mechanism

9/30/2020 #180

Day-102 "The Little Things-2"

You think they don't mean much
But they often do

You think they won't change much
But they often can

They are actions and reactions
They are emotions and devotions

They can be happy, gracious and kind
They can be sad, bad and unkind

They can take hostage your mind
In imperfect times

They can release your bonds
Put rainbows in your days

They are the tiniest of things
A single word
Stated in good faith
A misplaced word
Unkindly said

The loss of something dear
A misplaced key
A routine gone wrong
A glass of wine spilled

They often pierce your soul
They can change your life
Put it on hold

They can cleanse your mind
Sparkle like diamonds
Let it sing joy
You never know
What will come your way
On any one day
Shout out "Hooray"!
And see what may

It's all those little things
That change our days
As they often do

9/30/2020 #181

Day-102 "Will I be Me"

As I approach
The valley of despair

I cannot wait
To get on my way

I cannot wait
To see how far I've come
For I'll be halfway there
Is my foundation strong?
Will it stand the tide?
Am I one step away or two?

Will the winter storms
Flood my brain?

Will the spring rains
Grow flowers in my brain?

Will the summer sun
Bake my soul?

Will the autumn harvest
Change my ways?

When will my "JOY" bridge be complete?
Will it be tomorrow or the day after?
When will it reach the other side?
Will I be me when it is complete?
9/30/2020 #182

Day-102 "Rise up"

Hello it's me
Rise up you silly bum
Wash the dust from your eye
It is a new day

Rise up you silly bum
Wash the dust from your eye
It is a new day
Time to grab your pen

Wash the dust from your eye
It is a new day
Time to grab your pen
Spill ink upon this page

It is a new day
Time to grab your pen
Spill ink upon this page
Create lines of great repute
Paint a smile on someone's face

Rise up you silly bum
Rise up!

9/30/2020 #183

Day-102 "A Bucket of Joys"

I found a bucket today
It was full of Joys
I tried to name them all
But I was always one short

No matter how hard
I tried
I named and named
I counted and counted

Perhaps one hundred times
But I was always one short

I really don't understand why
I was always one shy

Did I misplace one?
Or did someone lie
I wondered why
It's not a sin
To be one short
For I just found it today
Was this bucket mine first or
Someone else's?

Who stole this Joy?
I want to know why
I think I will try
One more time
To fill this bucket of joys
To find the end of these lines

                         9/30/2020 #184

Day-109 " Heigh Ho!

Heigh Ho!
The West wind blows
Chasing dreams across the plains
Carrying us home
On clouds of glee

Heigh Ho!
The North wind blows
Chilling the bones
Of young and old
Light a fire
And let it glow

Heigh Ho!
The South wind blows
Warming the earth
Turning all
A glowing green

Heigh Ho!
The East wind blows
Harvests abound
Rejoice in our bounty
Sing Joys to the World

Heigh Ho!
Let the Four Winds Blow
Carry us home
On clouds of glee

                        10/6/2020 #185

Day-109 "In Search of Dopamine"

She had an unusual name
It was really hard to explain
Whenever near
She flooded my brain
With sensual thoughts

I couldn't define
This Dopamine
She was never quite mine
But like a glass of wine
She set my sails
To cascading tales

It was more than love
This Dopamine
I never could claim
Without any fame
Forever mine

A simple touch
Was but a flame
Locked up
Inside my heart
This Dopamine
One day she left
Without a goodbye
I think it a sin
This Dopamine

How crazy it is
These droplets of sin
Erased with a tonic and gin

Come back! Come back!
Oh, Delilah my love

10/6/2020 # 186

Day-110 "A Village Without A Name"

There once was a village
Without a name
The people therein
Thought and thought
They pondered and pondered
But couldn't come up with a name
To call their place

One day a stranger passed by
And stopped and asked why
There was no name for this place
It seems such a charming place
A very captivating place

Are you sure you haven't a name for this place
A name would make it great
And Great would make a Great name
For this village without a name

To which the villagers responded
Who are you to name our place?
And why would we want to be Great
When we are fine
The way we are?

To this the stranger replied
You can't be Great
Unless you have a Great name

People will come from miles around
To visit your Great little village
Called Great

This challenged the villagers
Some thought it was Great
To be named Great
While some thought it a mistake
If something went frightfully wrong

    So

They thought and they thought
They fought and they fought
They cried and they lied
But it wasn't a name
They all could claim
It split them apart
They all threw rocks
For years, this went on

Then one day a child stood
And asked them why
Why there were so many rocks in the road
So many crosses on the hill
Empty desks in the schools
Why this living hell
Just for a name

    So

They thought and they thought
Yet they couldn't explain
The disease in their brains
Who was right and who was wrong
The sky all dark and gray
The place that once had no name
Now, no one came
It wasn't so Great
To live in Great

The child then asked
Why call it anything at all

It doesn't have to have a name
It's just a space where
You can live without fame
It isn't a game
That one should claim

        So

They deliberated and speculated
They meditated and mitigated
They colluded
And finally concluded
That all would be Great
If they gave up that name
How Happy they could be if
They didn't have to be "Great"

10/7/2020 #187

This is a metaphorical synopsis of the current state of affairs that this country is stumbling and blundering through.

Day-111 "Rock Star"

I want to be a rock star
On the moon
Sing songs with the galaxies
In my yellow submarine
Take a rocket to earth
On Sunday after church
I want to be a Rock Star
In my lover's dreams

10/7/2020 #188

Day-111 "Up High"

I see you
High up in the sky
Gliding so effortlessly
It seems without a care
I know you wonder why
We down here often cry

Won't you come down
And tell us how you live
Without a care
So high up in the sky

Why are you so
Much more happy than
We down here
Think we are?

Sure, I'll tell you why
I so effortlessly fly

It's because the sky is free
The air I breathe is crystal clear
The breeze carries me
To sights unseen by human eyes

I require no money
But am not poor
And have no plans for war

I speak no evil
Of those who I oppose

I carry no hate
Into a new day

I neither build castles in the sand
Nor desire a loftier place

I take life for what it is
A moment in the sun

I love all those I meet
No matter their creed
Regardless their seed
To all in need

I require no more
Than what I need

That is why
I am more happy
Than you think you are

Take it from me
Following these thoughts
Will carry your soul
To a life unseen
Up High
Up here in the sky

10/8/2020 #189

Day-111 "Caring"

Let's pen a note to someone we miss
Make a call to someone who's lost a friend
Sit with a frail friend for an hour or so
Tell someone they did a great job
Tell your lover how gorgeous she is

It will make them feel good
Put a joy in their day
It will make you feel good
Put a joy in your day

Let's go caring today

                                              10/8/2020 #190

Day-111 "Tricks"

I learned a new trick today
It was a most exciting thing
I wondered why it just came now

It wasn't a card trick
Or a slight of hand

I didn't play it on anyone
For I am such a bore

It set me free
It tickled my spine

Sent endocrines
Clear to my toes

Without a doubt
It touched her soul
When she returned my Smile
Just Smile my friends
Just Smile

                                        10/8/2020 #191

Day-111 "Violent Storm"

A violent storm was brewing
Deep within his brain
The winds of change
 Blistering his soul
The waves pounding
Against his skull

Why me? Why me?
He cried
Never once have I lied
Never once have I not tried

> *It cannot be denied*
> *That never once have you lied*
> *And never once have you not tried*
> *The battle for your soul*
> *Is fraught with pride*
> *From deep inside*
> *You have to let it go*

But why? But why?
He cried

> *You're not that important*
> *Said the man in the sky*
> *Just flip the eggs*
> *And put a little jelly on the side*

                                        10/8/2020 #192

ENJOYMENTS

The following are poems about enjoyments. Things that people do that bring them joy.

Day-112 "The Gardener-2"

She planted seeds
In the spring
Daffodils, greens and beans

She tenderly labored
Tilling the soil
Hoeing the rows
Nourishing their needs

She named these
Children of the soil
Magnificent, Brilliant and Amazing
For they were Heaven sent

Their unexplainable explosions
Bringing her inexplicable joys

No greater honor
Than to be a gardener
A gardener of the soul

She planted seeds
In the spring

10/9/2020 #193

Day-112 "Mountain Climber"

He climbed a mountain today
To catch a sunrise
To taste the mountain air
To gaze across distant peaks
To be as high as eagles fly
To catch a star falling from the sky
To see what was on the other side
Once is never enough

                                                  10/9/2020 #194

Day-112 "The Reader"

Off the shelf they fly
Into the hands of you and I

Under covers late at night
In front of a fire on a winter's day

On a beach chair on a sunny day
In a plane across the sky

On a blanket in Central Park
Sipping a glass of wine when it's dark

Novels of love
And sinful lust

Poems of life
And rhyming lines

Politics and manuscripts
Crimes and mysterious plots

Magazines and newsprint
Letters of love and Johnny I'm gone

There is always time to
Read a few lines
Even though
They may not rhyme

                              10/9/2020 #195

Day-113 "The Dancers"

Swirling and twirling
The Cha- Cha- Cha
Two lovers meet
And dance as one
On a floor
Of crystal-clear ice

Bow legged cowboys
In Stetson hats
Ladies in Justin's
And ass fitting jeans
Dancing the two-step
In two-steps too
Girls in a line
Will be just fine

Bumping and Grinding
Jumping and Jerking
Rappers on the floor
Drumbeats and
Baseball caps askew
The beat goes on

Pelvis to Pelvis
Let it be Elvis
As you rumble
To the Rumba

Jumping and leaping
Soaring through the air
The grace of a swan
None to compare

Was poetry in motion
The Pas de chat
The Arabesque
The Penchee and Echappe
Don't ask me to explain
I never took French

                                          10/10/2020 #196

Day-113 "Players"

Our Gladiators
In plastic armor
Step on the field
Coming to kill
The victor the spoils
The turf survives
Hurray from the fans

A receiver down
A crooked nose bleeds
A stretcher deployed
Hurray for the hit

A long pass caught
A touchdown scored
Give me five
Way up high
Hurray for the score

A back runs free
Away from the guy
Who weighs
Three hundred and three

Hurray for the back
Whose five foot two
Who's the meanest
One of all

Hurray for the linebacker
Who put the Q-back
On his ass

Hurray! Hurray!
For the white dude
With a golden arm
Who fires cannonballs
For fifty yards

We jump with glee
When we win the score
How happy we are

Hurray for our gladiator boys
To the team we cheer
Let's have another beer

10/10/2020 #197

Day-113 "The Fisherman"

Cheers to the man
Who likes to fish
With a fly
In a mountain stream

Cheers to the boy
Who hooks a fish
On his very first try

Cheers to grandpa
Who untangles
The hook
That caught his ear

Cheers to the man
Who fished all day long
Drove home without a catch

Cheers to the wife
Who packs his gear
Without a beer

Cheers to the bartender
Who has to measure
The fish that was not caught

Cheers to the men
Who don't give a damn
If they catch or throw away
Was time well spent
On a sunny day

                        10/10/2020 #198

Day-114 "The Singers"

Oh, to be Bon Jovi
Living out joys
On a "Bed of Roses"

Or

Helen Reddy
Forever strong
"I am woman"
Watch me grow

Janis J
"Me and Bobby McGee"

Their voices
Sing chorus lines
Engraved in time

Their songs
Tell of lives
In nursery book lines

Melodies that rhyme
Exposing their souls
Telling their lives

Oh, to be a song
That would be sung
By a voice
As heavenly as those

Oh, to be a singer
With a melodious voice
Would be
The purest of Joys

Why can't we all be singers?
As heavenly as those
Is that too much to ask?

                        10/11/2020 #199

Day-114 "Just Sing"

Some sing praises
Some sing the blues
Some sing rock and roll
Some sing rap
Some sing country
Some sing just to be singing

Some sing in showers
Some sing in barber shop choirs
Some sing in smoke filled bars
Some sing in their lover's ear
Some sing just to be singing

Some sing when they are happy
Some sing when they are trying to forget
Some sing when they are in love
Some sing just to be singing

Why can't we all sing?
Is that too much to ask?   10/11/2020 #200

Day-114 "The Poet"

He who writes a great line
And makes it rhyme
Will live in time

                        10/11/2020 #201

Day-115 "Finding Joys"

They surround you
They inspire you
They cry with you
They laugh with you

They hide behind closed doors
And in closet drawers

They climb with the sun
On mountain peaks

They simmer with friends
On a summer's eve
A deer in a meadow
Feeding her fawn

A cat on a pillow
With a big yawn

A man holding a rose
Knocking on your door

They swim in lakes
With nothing on

They can be anything
As long as they please

Yours to behold
Even in the darkest of days

Open your mind
They are easy to find

                                                          10/12/2020 #202

Day-116 "Joys"

Hold fast to your joys
For if Joys die
Broken is your life
It cuts like a knife

Hold fast to your joys
For when joys are lost
Your life becomes a barren field
Covered in snow

10/13/2020 #203

This poem is a parody of "Dreams" by the famous poet, Langston Hughes. I substituted Joys for Dreams with a few twists to make it mine. Dreams is such a wonderful poem that it sits upon my desktop and I read it every day.

Day-116 "Seeing Joy"

Are you Joy rich
Or Joy poor

The many ways
You see joy
Is but a reflection

It can be a rock
In a little boy's eye
If it skips just right

It can be a dream
In a little girl's eye
Of kings and queens
And fairy tale scenes

It can be a baby
In a mother's eye
Dressed in pink

It can be a boy
In a father's eye
Growing into a man

In many
It is but a scene
Like sun
Through a forest green

To some
A moment of peace
When they discover the truth

To most
They are different
But much the same
They all put a
Sparkle in your soul
And a smile on your face

10/13/2020 #204

Day-117 "Every Night I pray"

Every night
I pray for Peace

Every night
I pray for Love

Every night
I pray for Joy

Without Peace
There can be no Love

Without Love
There can no Joy

Without Joy
There is neither Peace nor Love

If you have Peace
You can have Love

If you have Love
You can have Joy

If you have Joy
You will have
Peace and Love

Every night
I'm on bended knee

                        10/14/2020 #205

Day-117 "Dreaming"

Every night I Dream
That Joy will come
With the rising sun

That multitudes will follow
Singing joyful songs
Into the setting sun.

10/14/2020 #206

Live Joyfully

My thought for this day is "Live a Good Life". In order to live a good life, it must be garnished with peace and love. A good life cannot be tainted by either hate or repression for they create negative thoughts and actions. In order to overcome these negatives, you have to work at it. You have to find a little joy in all that you do and all that surrounds you. That is one of the primary purposes of all that I have written in this unending task to write 365 poems of joyful and positive thoughts.

So many poets write about all the sadness that exists in this world. Even though it is good poetry I find it depressing and in lieu of the task that I have set for myself it tarnishes my thoughts. It makes it extremely difficult to write about "Joy" when the world is full of negative thoughts and actions. Regardless, I am compelled to keep at this task in hopes that I will accomplish my goal. In the meantime I hope that you have enjoyed these few poems about all the enjoyments that are out there waiting to be discovered. My thoughts to you on this day are found in the following poem.

Day-118 "Live Joyfully"

They drain the brain
Tarnishing your soul
Until the dawn alights

Persistent they are
Creeping around behind closed doors
On Halloween nights

Do not despair
Your soldiers are many
Pull out your sword
And chase them away

Tis much easier than you think
The power of joy
Can rule your day.

Let loose your enjoyments
Fly with them across the sky

Happy are the many who
Have a joyful life
"Vivez joyeux"

Have a good day my friend
It's time to move on.

10/15/2020 #207

Day-120 "Little Barefoot Boy"

Cherish the moment
Little barefoot boy
Play in your sandbox
Forever today

Dig and scoop
Mold and shape
Build your castle high
Fill the moot
With water from a
Garden hose

Play your game of
Knights and thieves
Climb the turret rope
And save the Queen

When you are done
Squash it with your foot
For there will surely come
Another day
My Little barefoot boy

                                        10/16/2020 #208

Day-120 "Little Barefoot Girl"

Spinning and twirling
Amongst the trees
Across the green, green grass
She danced
My little barefoot girl

The early morning rays
Glistening off her hair
Her tippy toes
Gliding through the air
A ballerina in flight
My little barefoot girl

Little squirrels stopped
And watched
Tiny birds sang
In branches high
A puppy dog yipped
And ran away

I held her hand and danced with her
I swung her high above my head
Breaking her fall in outstretched arms
Squealing with laughter
My little barefoot girl

A morning from heaven
We both enjoyed

Oh, yes
That was the day
She's much older now
Let me remember her
That way
My little barefoot girl
As I give her away   10/17/2020 #209

Day-120 "Daydream Boys"

Walking along a dusty trail
Guitar slung over his back
Blue jeans and old
Cowboy boots

Whistling a tune
Strolling along
Dreaming a song
Only the trees
Could hear

Hey little boy
Won't you let me
Be with you today
I'll listen as you strum
That old guitar
We'll write a song
That all will sing

Walking along a city street
Basketball in hand
Gym shorts and old
Tennis shoes

Bouncing the ball
Dreaming a game
As he went along
Only the asphalt
Could see

Hey little boy
Won't you let me
Be with you today
We'll shoot hoops
Until she calls us home
Michael Jordan you'll surely be

Two boys in worlds apart
Dreaming of lives they want to be
One a singer wanting to sing
One a player wanting to play

Is that too much to ask
Of dreams they want to be
My little daydream boys

                        10/18/2020 #210

Day-123 "Fishing"

Hey buddy
Won't you let me
Be with you today
I'll bait the hook
Untangle the line
We'll catch a fish
And throw it back

I'll tell you stories
Of when I was
A little boy

                        10/19/2020 #211

Day-123 "Writing Love Songs"

He was all the things
I wanted to be
A poet writing love songs
In the stillness of the dawn

Harvesting his memory
For places, plots and scenes
Amplifying interpolations
In lines that sometimes rhyme

Oh, to be a poet
On a winter's day
The wind blowing hard
Against the windowpane

Thoughts emerging
Of a springtime morn
A sparrow up high
Greeting the morning rays

Coffee pot brewing
Bacon sizzling

A lover under cover
Awaiting
A morning kiss

Oh, the many words
I would love to pen
These precious moments
To never end

A poet writing love songs
In the stillness of the dawn.

10/19/2020 #212

Day-124 "Little Words"

Little words
Can change your mind

Little words
Can make you cry

Little words
Can make you laugh
What are little words for?

Little words
Can change your life

Little words
Could make you mine

                              10/20/2020 #213

Day-124 "Moments"

Look around
These moments are yours
Never to have again
Take a snapshot
Place them in a rhyme

Treasure them forever
Store them in a hallowed hall
Uncover them whenever
You need a little pleasure

                              10/20/2020 #214

Day-124 "Brain Waves"

If your name is Sad
We'll paint roses in the sand

If your name is Mad
We'll help you find another home

If your name is Happy
You can come and go
Any old time you please

10/20/2020 #215

Day-125 "Ain't Got No Blues"

Ain't got no Blues
In this joint
Ain't got no heart

Ain't got no Blues
In my heart
Ain't got no horn

Ain't got no Blues
In my horn
Ain't got no soul

Ain't got no Blues
In my soul
Ain't got no house

Ain't got no Blues
In my house
Ain't got no Love

Ain't got no heart
Ain't got no horn
Ain't got no soul
Ain't got no house
Ain't got no love
Ain't got no Blues

10/21/2020 #216

Day-127 "Serenity"

We met along a wooded path
Where upon we strolled
Throughout our pasts

We sat upon a rock
By a stream
Running to the sea
Slow down she said
Slow down

I played a flute
On a mountain side
A little deer came near
Savor the sight she said
Savor the sight

We strolled along a beach
Chased the waves
In bare feet
Savor the rhythm she said
Savor the rhythm

We watched a sunset
On a mountain perch
Until it sank into the sea
Savor the beauty she said
Savor the beauty

We gazed at the stars
On a cloudless night
The moon shining bright
Savor the thought she said
Savor the thought

Two bodies entwined
Long before dawn
Slow down she said
Slow down

                                              10/23/2020 #217

Day-128 "Find a New Joy"

When you can no longer
Climb that mountain
Find your calm

When you can no longer
Win that war
Find your peace

When you can no longer
Laugh with the crowd
Find your compassion

When you can no longer
Speak well of another
Find your kindness

When you can no longer
Find the end of a day
Find a new Joy

                                              10/24/2020 #218

Day-129 "Life's Melodrama"

Life is but a melodrama

    Of

This's and that's

    Of

Ups and downs

    Of

Ins and outs

    Of

Boos and Hisses

    Of

Tears and Laughs

    Of

Roses and Thistles

    Of

Me's and My'ys

    And

Oh my God's

    10/25/2020 #219

Day-129 "Sexy Letters"

What you ask is the
Sexiest letter in the alphabet

I say the E...
For its erotic desire
It's always on fire
Sure to inspire

Start with Eros and Erogenous
Journey through Erotic
To Ecstasy
Onward to Ecstatic
By way of Enticing and Exciting.
Throw in a little Elation and Engaging
As well as Eager and Enchanting and
You have a letter that is always
Enjoyable, Endowed and Exquisitely
On fire.

         10/25/2020 #220

Day-129 "S is Sexy Too"

I Thought of S
As being Sexy too
For it is Sensual, Sweet and Sensitive.
It is Special, Stunning and Satisfying.
As well as Snug, Soft and Spicy
It can be Spirited and Strong
Spectacular, Surprising and Sensational
Sometimes you forget
How Sexy S it is

         10/25/2020 #221

Day-129 "The Letter T"

The Letter T
Can be quite Tasteful and Touching
Thrilling, Talented and Tender
It is often Tingling and Ticklish
Tantalizing and Tempting
Tasty and Terrific
But more often than not
Treasured

                                                    10/25/2020 #222

Day-129 "Other Love Letters"

A is Alluring, Adoring and Appealing
It is Attractive, Amorous and Amazing.
It is Adorable, Adventurous and Awesome

B is Beautiful, and Blissful
Blazing, Beaming and Breathtaking

C is Calming and Climatic.
Cozy, Comfy and Cherished.
Content, and Complete

And Yes,
F is Funny too

This brings me to
            "The End"
Yet there are so many more

                                                    10/25/2020 #223

Day-129 "A Sheet of Paper"

This sheet of paper
Sometimes cries and sometimes lies
Is often full of laughs and sighs
Tells stories of times and lives

It beckons in the dark
Waves in the afternoon light
Bleeds your brain dry
When it doesn't rain

It is but a sheet of paper
Waiting to be etched
With your chisel of lead

Praise the day when
The adventures are many
Let them rest
When the days are short

It is but a sheet of paper
Awaiting the touch
Of your brush
Stroke it gently
There are many pages
Yet to be writ

10/25/2020 #224

Day-129 "Girders of Love"

I ventured back today
To see if I could lay girders on the piers
That will bridge the "Valley of Despair"
Through which a raging river flows

I found the river running fast and furious
Covid-19 hiding behind boulders and
Along the shore and up the valley walls
There were fires in the forests
Landscapes charred
Two kings waring
Black men dying
People marching
Suicides rising
Mothers trying
Children crying
Schools closing
The "River"................ Furious!

What an ungodly sight
Was my task too difficult?
Is my work rusting away?
Will these girders of Love
Ever stand the test of time
Can we build this bridge?
Will the "Valley of Despair" ever be breeched?

10/25/2020 #224

In my quest to build a bridge across the "Valley of Despair" I am concerned that it may never be completed no matter how hard we try. Perhaps it is just a dream. Regardless, if it keeps us sane in these troubled times then it will have accomplished most of my objectives. I would encourage you to go back and read poems 2, 5, 15, 59 and 100. They all deal with this arduous task. However, it is also time to pack up my pen and journey on.

Day-130 "Moving On"

Days are shortened
By the northern winds
Time to pack our bags
And journey on

Many miles to travel
Before we rest
A new dawn breaking
Will put us to the test

Treasures left behind
Are but of the mind
New Adventures
We'll embrace

We'll conquer all
With love and peace
Painted on our adobe walls

Valleys deep
And rivers wide
Are ours to conquer
With a smile

The clock has struck
The bell has rung
It's time to move on
My friend
It's time to move on

         10/26/2020 #225

Day-130 "Brave Men"

Oh, brave men of the sea
Tell me what it is you've seen
What treasures have you brought
From lands afar

From oceans wide
We've seen pyramids in the sky
Gorgeous mountains standing high
Herbal plants and palm tree leaves
Native peoples loving free

Oh, brave men of the sky
Please look me in the eye
Tell me how high you fly
What lies beyond
That which we see

The galaxies wide
We cannot lie
Man will never see
We can only spy
But cannot buy
A billion solar lights
Surely God is one of these

Oh, brave men of the streets
Why do you march
In times like these
What is the change
You hope to change

It is never mean
To march in the streets
We march for Justice, Peace and Equality
For the men who sail the seas
And those who reach for stars
To be alike you and me.

                           10/26/2020 #226

Day-131 "Sweet Dreams"

Invading your brain
Capturing your thoughts
A lava lamp of spiritual scenes
A kaleidoscope of revolving doors
Paintings in yellows, reds and greens
Words in rhymes and blacks and whites

A woman and her pen
A man and his brush
A child and a toy
So soft the pillow
In the dark before dawn

                           10/27/2020 #227

Day-131 "Priming the Brain"

From your treasure chest of words
Pull out one that makes you laugh
Another that makes you smile

As you go about your morning tasks
Repeat them each one hundred times

Fantastic, Fantastic, Fantastic
Awesome, Awesome, Awesome

Enjoy the rush these words bring
Joyful the flush that overcomes
They're sure to reset your mind
Priming it for the coming day
Tomorrow try another and another and another

                                              10/27/2020 #228

Day-131 "No Matter What the Scene"

Place your easel on the ground
Anywhere will be just fine
No one will really mind

Make this your spot
For the day.

Intrusions will surely come
No matter what the scene

Is yours to choose rather
To complain or strike them through

It is but your signature
You place upon the cloth

Yours to entertain
Those who pass you by
No matter what the scene

10/27/2020 # 229

Day-132 "They Laughed"

I jumped and
Clicked my heels
And they laughed

I spun around
And fell on the floor
And they laughed

I did a summersault
In the rain
And they laughed

I turned a cartwheel
On a garden path
And they laughed

They thought me
Crazy
When they laughed

They thought me
Insane
When they laughed

Little do they know
I think them
Quite jealous

If they could
They would
They don't even
Know my name

My name is "Joy"
I lurk in the woods
And only come out
When darkness
Covers the moon

Yes,

You can be sad
But you can also
Be glad

Just make the glad
More than the sad

So,

Throw away your shoes
And dance a jig

I'll teach you the Bumfuzzle
And the Hullabaloo

There is always
Time for a good
Laugh.

Even when you are
Jealously insane

10/28/2020 #230

Day-134 "Gems "

Lay bare the
"Louvre" in your brain
Beauty in a frame
Traces of Michelangelo and
Leonardo too

It's there to tease
Whenever you please
Even on a summer's breeze

Read the brochure
It's sure to allure
Take a grand tour
Speaks the danseur

Pull wide the curtain
Behold the stage
As actors proclaim
Their love for fame
Let them entertain
Throughout the day
From the "Louvre" in your brain

          10/29/2020 # 231

Day-135 "Halloween Night"

They mean to shock
Awaken with my thoughts
On Halloween night

Little ghosts and goblins
At my front door
Begging to tease
Candy please

Show me a trick
Or give me a treat
No witch's brew
For I will surely stew

Skeletons in flight
Hanging from trees
Spiders and snakes
Behind dungeon doors

They growl in the dark
Scream bloody hell
Little monsters
They surely are

Away she flew
On a broom for two
Giving a ride
To a horseman's skull

Her pointy nose
And crackling voice
Gave rise
To the graves as
They came alive

An army of Monsters
Vampires, and Zombies
Draculas and Werewolves
Came marching down my street

Knock, Knock, Knock
Knocking on my front door
I'll serve them
A bloody delight
A witch's brew
Mixed in a stew
From the bowels of my crypt

A taste of cider
And a cookie too
They love to scare
I love to treat
On Halloween night

10/31/2020 #232

Day-136 'Changing of the Guard"

Summer days well past their prime
A changing of the guard
Took place last night at two

Dark days of winter loom
Leaves in golden hue
Foretell the coming storms

Warm your bed with woolen cloth
Pull the flannels from your chest
Fill your hearth with fresh cut logs

Soon the snow will fall
Glazing windows with its frost
Sleigh bells ringing cross the vale
Squirrels scurrying for their cache
Foxes burrowing in their nests
Bears snoozing long to rest

V shapes in the sky
The geese are flying south
Listen as they pass us by

We'll wait for their return
In the flowering spring

Pull your stocking cap
Way down tight
Ready your snowshoes
For a morning hike

With your heart felt breath
Script a verse
On a window glass

Telling the world
How much you love
The changing of the guard.

11/1/2020 # 233

Day- 138 "Toasts"

Here is to the woman
Who bore your life
Who sings with you
Who holds you tight
Whenever you need
Thank you, Mother dear,

Here is to the man
Who gave you life
Who makes you laugh
Who wipes your tears
When you are sad
Thank you dear ol' Dad

11/3/2020 #234

Day 139 "For You Ladies"

Don't you know
It is a sin
To drink a gin
Without a him

Don't you know
It is a crime
When in your prime
You haven't the time

Don't you know
That when you lie
You cannot cry
When he leaves you dry

Don't you know
That when he pleads
He's a little child
With draconian needs.

                                            11/3/2020 #235

Day-139 "Roses and Rainbows"

Roses and Rainbows
Melodies and Poetry

Butterflies and Eskimo pies
Desert skies and mountain top highs

Tasty treats and Fantastic Feats
Moonshine and Ruby red wine

Hallelujahs and Halloo boo-ya's
Heavenly's and Delightfully's

These are the things we see
These are who we be
When we are happy and free

Roses and Rainbows
Desert skies and mountain top highs

                                            11/4/2020 #236

Day-141 "Bird Man"

There was an old man
Who came to the street
Every day at three

Feeding pigeons
Crusty old bread
And popcorn treats

From steeples and rooftops
They flew
Fluttering and cooing
Snipping and pecking
At his feet for a daily treat

Quite a crowd he drew
We watched in awe
This delightful scene
The multitude grew large

When

Into a rage he flew
As a lady ran through
Stepping on one
Away they took wing

He cursed and burst
Heaving his treats
At the lady in retreat

She didn't recall
What she had done
She thought them just birds
At his feet on the street

He ranted and raved
Repentant she was
Much too late
To extinguish his flame

The pigeons flew back
Attacking his sack
All scatted about
On that old cobble stoned street

So distraught was he
He fell to his knees
Leaving a trail of tears on that
Old cobble stoned street

          11/4/2020 #237

I watched in awe that day in Vienna as the old man shed his joy. However, I am sure he'll be back just like the pigeons, and we will once again enjoy his joy.

Day-145 "Rhapsody in Democracy"

They came running
To Lafayette Square
Blacks, Browns and Whites
Singing and cheering
They came to celebrate
The mighty man's dispose

No gas this time
No stomping steeds
No bashing clubs
No desecrations

Human beings
Young and old
Proclaiming their will
Rejoicing their faith
That good eventually reigns

The bands came marching
Trumpets blaring
Trombones bellowing
Drums pounding
Majorettes beaming

Stars and stripes
Waving proud
Defined the multitude
That gathered there

The people's court declared
The changing of the guard
Bells rang throughout the land
The mighty man disposed
They came to Lafayette Square

11/8/2020 # 238

Day-147 "Tid Bits-4"

Have you ever stood naked
In front of a mirror
And wondered why
They laughed at you?   11/10/2020 #239

Day- 147 "Tid Bits-5"

When all is right
You must fight
With all your might
To keep it right   11/10/2020 #240

Day -147 "Tid Bits-6"

We should often
Laugh at ourselves
For it is plain
That being vain
Is a losing disease   11/10/2020 # 241

Day-147 "Tid Bits-7"

I found it easier
To find a forest
Where there are no trees
Than change the will
Of a narcissistic soul   11/10/2020 # 242

It's been one week since our presidential election in which Joseph R. Biden defeated Mr. Trump. Yet Mr. Trump won't concede that he lost. What a sham. This does not speak well for our democracy.

Day-147 "Onward We March"

Onward we march
Looking for happier times
Searching our souls
For the betterment of mankind

It's ours to lead
Not to bleed
The cup of democracy's soul

Please God
Deliver us from
These solemn times
Bring merriment
Back in a rhyme
That we all can chime

Spew it out
There is no doubt
That we will rise
And fail again and again
But in the end
Peace will reign
And new stars will rise
With the morning tide

> 11/10/2020 #243

I'm trying to get myself back in a much happier mood. It has been fraught with many arrows to my soul. I can't help but believe that these times will be over soon and that a change in leadership will pave a much brighter path, and that COVID 19 will soon find its page in the history of mankind.

Day-147 "Digging for Nuts"

Oh, to be a squirrel
Digging for nuts
Outside my window space

Pouncing from here to there
Flying from branch to branch
Digging and pawing
Tail twitching and jerking

Eyes looking
In my window glass
As if I, a stranger
Stealing his buried prize

Perhaps I'll tease him
With crumbs from a jar
Will he find them I wonder?
A feast to enjoy
On this snow-covered day

Come quick
He's found the loot
Cracking a smile
On this old wooden face
Inside my window space

Oh, to be a squirrel
Just digging for nuts

11/10/2020 #244

Day-147 "This Old Car"

This old car
Is hard to turn
No grease on the wheels
To smooth its flight

Lift my eyes
To the morning light
Let it shine bright
On my old metal hood

Take a page
From an old "Hot Rod" mag
Stuff it in the glove box
Read it later
In classroom time

Rock and Roll
With KOMA
Cruising down the
Highway of time

Bobby socks and
High school jocks
45's in a juke box

Greasy hair and
Cigarette packs
Sock hops and Bee bops
Betty Lou and Suzie Cue

The 50's coming back
In midnight dreams
Peddle to the metal
This old car is
Hard to turn off

11/10/2020 # 245

Day-148 "A Beautiful Line"

Such a beautiful line
Full of love
Overflowing with compassion
Full of passion

Pulsating with sensitivity
Full of serenity
Touchingly thoughtful

How one thought
How one word
How one line
Can change the world

"I appreciate you"
Such a beautiful line
Let's learn to use it
Much, much more often

11/11/2020 #246

I took this line from an email from Melony Fitzwater a Senior VP of Security National Trust Company. It says so much and should be used much more often by all of us.

Day-150 "Simplicity"

Sometimes the simplest

Of things mean the most

A pat on the back

A kind word

A smile

The wink of an eye

A hug

A blue sky

Sometimes the simplest

Of things mean the most

11/13/2020 #247

Day- 150 "Ballad of Billy Joe Bob"

There once was a man named Billy Joe Bob
Who lived in a town named Hill Billy Mill
It seemed everyone had three names
He was a man that few cared to claim

A man with three names who could care less
He was a mess. I'm sure you can see why
Not knowing who you are can be quite a test.

Was it Billy Joe Bob or Joe Billy Bob I'm really not sure?
It could have been Bob Billy Joe that rode
Into Hill Billy Mill on that hot summer day
On a filly named Milly Mo Billy carrying
A case of whisky from Frisky, San Frisky.

"Try Singing this when you ~~you're~~ haven't a clue"
Not knowing who you are can be quite a test

Stinking of that fine brew Billy Joe Bob
Flew off Ol' Milly Mo Billy and handed the reigns to a lady
Called Tipsy Times Two who hadn't a clue with what to do
With that cantankerous old filly called Milly Mo Billy.   Well,...
Ol' Milly Mo Billy was quite confused when Tipsy
Times Two called her Billy Mo Milly. She reared in the air
And her hoofs of steel came crashing down on poor Ol' Billy Joe Bob,
Or was it Joe Billy Bob, as we were quite confused from the whiskey
from Frisky, we drank when we laid him to rest on top of Hill Billy
Hill.

"Try Singing this when you haven't a clue"
Not knowing who you are can be quite a test.
                              11/13/2020 #248

I felt that I need a little more cheer in this formidable task, so I went to my book "The World Through My Window" and pulled this one out. Which is supposed to lead into the next poem.

Day-150 "Beer Belly Bob's"

As you might guess
In this little town called "Hill Billy Mill"
There just happened to be a quaint
Little place called "Beer Belly's Bar"
That was owned by a feller
Named Beer Belly Bob who
Looked much the same as
The name of his bar

Well, "Beer Belly's Bar" was
The corner stone of Hill Billy Mill
If you wanted to know something
Or if you wanted everyone to know something
You drank at Beer Belly's Bar
And stayed for as long as you could remain erect.
Or was that erectile?

Well, Beer Belly's Bar was where you could find
Tipsy Times Two most afternoons and
Typically, Tipsy Times Two was two times tipsy by two.

And by the time most of the local yokels came drinking
She was out for the count.

Actually, Tipsy Times Two was also the local hairdresser
As well as the bartender in this quaint little town.

Of course, unbeknownst to the local yokels Beer Belly Bob
And Tipsy Times Two had quite a thing going.
Chuckle, Chuckle, Ha-Ha.......

Of course, they had their differences
Tipsy Times two liked whiskey from old Frisky San Frisky
While Beer Belly Bob craved buckets of beer and
Canisters of Skoal.

Tipsy Times Two loved ruby red lipstick and bubble gum too
She also had a tattoo we won't mention where;
But for a green back she just might give you a peek.

On the other hand, Beer Belly Bob wore wife beater T's
And bell bottom jeans that showed off his plumber's ass.
Now that was not a pretty scene.

Did I mention they were cousins?

As you might guess they sometimes had their differences
Which required the assistance of Sheriff Johnny Come Lately
To mitigate their disparities. More often than not one or the other
Won an overnight stay in the local calaboose.

It was a Friday afternoon, somewhere around 3:00, and Beer Belly's
Bar Was pretty damn busy and Tipsy Times Two was nowhere to be
found.

The pool tables were full and bustling with cheer. The bar was packed
elbow to elbow or gun-barrel to gun-barrel, a much more fitting
acronym to be sure.

As you can imagine Beer Belly Bob was in quite a stew
For he couldn't keep up pouring the brew with Tipsy Times Two
nowhere to be found.

When through the door busted that cantankerous old filly called Milly
Mo Billy. Or was it Billy Mo Milly? Astride old Milly Mo Billy sat
Tipsy Time Two in her "Lady Godiva" gear and stiletto heels waving
her forty-eights while brandishing a 44.

A few shots through the roof of that old bar caused many an eyeball to
pop out of their sockets like exploding packs of Rickenbacker popcorn.

Now that was just about enough to scare the Webby-Jibbies out of
every gun-totin' liberal in the bar as they dove for cover under every
table and chair with a few diving through the plate glass window next
to the door.

As if on cue Old Milly Mo Billy reared and flew across the floor chasing poor Beer Belly Bob around the room cornering him up against the bar. When the loudest scream there ever was heard rang out through the rafters of that crusty old saloon.

"You no good, Cheatin', Snuff Spittin, Siberian Sheep Herder"; Iffen I ever catch you foolin' round with Miss Bony Bones Boobies again old Milly Mo Billy and I'll drag your plumbers crack ass across those RR tracks out back and tar and feather you right there on the spot. And just so you know what you ain't gonna get no more, iffen you do, I want all your boys to see what you ain't gonna get and where my tattoo ends.

With that she stood up in the saddle giving her forty-eights one last jiggle and kicked old Milly Mo Billy in the side and with a grand "Hidy Ho"out the door they hurled. Or was that Milly Billy Mo?

11/13/2020 #249

Day-152 "The Joy Man"

It was the middle of July
And not a cloud in the sky
When out of the blue
The strangest man you ever did see
Came skipping and prancing
Down our cobblestoned street.

Dressed in strawberry-colored pants
A cape of yellows, reds and blues
And tinkle bell shoes.
Upon his head a jester's hat
In his hand a ten holed flute.

We stared in awe as
Magical rose-colored puffs
Rose from the ground
Wherever his feet did touch
And star like crystals flew
From that ten holed flute.

Was he a clown
Or a man from our
Medieval past?
On his face a mask
We could not tell.
We had certainly never
Seen such a comical sight.

As if on cue
The children flew
Out of portals and hatches;
From behind canisters and cans
Off teeter tots and jungle gym bars.
They dropped all they were doing
And began singing and laughing,
Skipping and prancing,

Twisting and twirling,
Following in step around the
Town square they went.

The sky turned a purple pinkish blue.
The town square Maple began to sway
And dance in the breeze.
Alley cats meowed and little dogs howled.
In steeple high a church bell clanged.

Mothers and fathers,
Sisters and brothers,
Uncles and aunts,
Cops and robbers,
Lovers and all others,
Hooked arms and fell in line.

Around and around they went
Till twilight began to yawn
And stars began to shine;
When suddenly we asked
Who was this man?
Who brought us so much joy?

We looked around and realized that
No one really knew.
So, we asked him to unmask.

To our surprise it
Was the Mayor of our town
All dressed up and gay
Spreading joy for all to enjoy.

All it takes is one little man
With a great big smile,
A magical touch and a heart of gold
To change the way we are.

11/15/2020 #250

Day-153 "Never Lost"

I went looking for Happy today
For he had run away
Nowhere to be found

Then there was Smiley
Who also ran away
Nowhere to be found

Poor little Glad
Was really mad
Wanting to hold my hand

We searched the fields
Behind our home

We tarried up and down
The street in front of our house

We looked in canisters and cans
Behind doors and under cars

The sky turned gray
Thunder doomed and lightning stuck
Tearing a hole inside our souls
Not knowing what to do
We ran inside and began to cry

The hail fell hard
On our tin thatched roof
The pounding unbearable
The fireplace cold
We held each other tight
When all of a sudden
There came a scratching
A scratching from our cellar door

What could it be said I
Speak softly said Little Glad

Could it be a ghost said I
Could it be a squirrel said Little Glad

I turned the latch
The hinges squeaked
The old door creaked
We fell to our knees
As into our arms flew our
Happy and Smiley.

The thunder stopped
The hail went away
The sun shone bright
It made us Happy and Smiley too
Little Glad and I

11/16/2020 #251

The moral of this story is that being Happy and Smiley are never lost. They are always there begging you to open your own cellar door before you run outside and look for more.

"A Change is Coming"

With these next few poems, I am going to write about the changing of the seasons. I am taking a few from my stockpile and will be adding a few new ones. The COVID 19 virus has reached a new stage. 100's of thousands are being infected and 1,000's are dying each day. There is certainly hope on the horizon with some very promising vaccines. This is indeed very good news. Hopefully, this reflects a changing of the season. It has been a long ten months and many are facing depression and COVID fatigue. Remembering my original intent was to write feel good poems. Maybe, just maybe the world will get a handle on this virus and we can all get back to living happy and meaningful lives. I'll leave you with the statistics that I wrote and sent to our local Gazette Newspaper. They titled it "Comparing Serious Statistics"

The intent of these statistics is to point out the fact that this virus is like fighting a war and that deaths due to this virus are little different than lives lost in war. There are numerous similarities that I will perhaps write about later.

Some quick stats:

America entered WWII on December 7, 1941, and closed out the war on September 2, 1945
Americans Killed in the war totaled 407,316
Average number killed per month: 8,485

COVID claimed its First Death in early February 2020
Total deaths to date: 247,370
Average number of COVID deaths per month to date: 24,737

Estimated time to reach 407,316 deaths in America from this date: 6.47 Months at 24,737 deaths per month. That is 824 per day.
If that isn't enough to scare the heck out of you nothing will. It's time to put on your Red Cross Pants and start wearing a mask.

(One of the problems with the above stats is that US deaths topped 1,700 per day yesterday)

Day-155 "Frost Fairies"

Come hither my child
Wipe the sleep
From your eyes
And leave the comfort
Of your bed.

Take my hand
And come with me
There is a mystical
Sight to behold
Outside our cabin door.

Quick!
Come to the window
See what has happened
In the dark of the night.

The world has turned to glass
The pine needles all turned to ice
The sage all glistening white
Like stars in the morning light.

> *What is it*
> *She whispered*
> *It's such a beautiful sight*
> *Yesterday it was all green*
> *How did this happen?*

Oh, my little one
It's magic
Brought to us
By little creatures of the night.

> *Creatures of the night?*
> *How can that be?*

Oh yes, my little one
I call them fairies
Tiny little angels
With wings that flicker
And flutter about.

They circle high
In the heavens above
And only come out on
Icy cold
Star lit nights.

They carry
Magical wands and
Packets of crystal diamonds
When it is just right
Just before light
They sprinkle them about.

They are as light
As feathers and cover
All the grasses
And all the trees
Even the noses
Of the deer in the meadow below.

They paint the world white
With brush strokes
From their wings
Making all things
Crystal bright.

When the sun peaks
Over the distant vale
They take their magical wands
And christen this sculpted scene
Leaving you a masterpiece
Of a thousand glistening stars.

With her face against the
Windowpane she said

    "I would like to paint that someday"

And the sun smiled
And I smiled
At the gift, the angels
Gave us that day

                        11/18/2020 #252

Day-155 "First Snow"

Holding hands, they watch
The sunlight rays
Diminish the stars
As gray clouds gather
On mountain high
To clothe the sky

The autumn air
Serenely quiet
Chilled by the
Steamy breath
From the Boreal plains

Downy feathers flutter
And dance about
Dressing pines and cedars
In crystalline pearls
A pristine sight for little girls

Outside the pane
An artist paints
A flip of her hand
A touch of her brush
A masterpiece appears
White topped mountains
Grow on garden posts
Little squirrels become like ghosts
A rocky ledge
Becomes a white hedge
A lady statue
Turns blue

The maestro taps his baton
And with a wave of his hand
Symphonic notes drift across the sky
Ballerinas swirl and twirl

The pines begin to bow
The cedars turn white
To Bolero's flight
Inside the cabin
The tick of a clock
A crackling fire
Is all that's heard
As downy feathers flutter
And dance about
Outside my windowpane

        11/18/2020 #253

Day-157 "A Winter's Day"

The nights are long and cold
Wrapped in blankets
On bear skinned rugs
And rocking chairs

Plenty of cider and
Christmas carols
To Bethlehem many
Make their way

Christmas tree all lit
Little ones staying up late
Spying on old St. Nick

Snowballs and slippery slopes
Show shoes and parka coats
Mugs of chocolate and brandy shots
A lover to keep you warm

Don't tell me there
Is nothing to do on a winter's day
Soon we'll be trading them
For a springtime rain
And tulips in Keukenhof

11/19/2020 #254

Day-157 "The Wreath of Life"

April came and brought spring rain
Thawing streams and fields of green

Sunlight rays awake the dawn
Mother Earth stretches and yawns

Frisky colts in paddocks play
Mother cows nursing their young

Tulips brighten Keukenhof
Famers plant their seeds and wait for rain

Summer heat blisters the soil
The days much longer now

Wind whispers through Bluestem grass
Meadowlarks sing their prairie songs

Skinny dipping in farmer's pond
Playing guitars on pickup beds

Row after row
Corn grows high over hill and vale

Ice cold tea in twilight hours
Couple rocking on bungalow porch

September calls the kids to school
Ferried off in yellow bus

Fall trees in glorious rust
Harvest time has come at last

We'll remember well this year
Thanksgiving time is near
The nights are long and cold

Coming soon those winter days
A Christmas wreath awaits
Grandpa and his sleigh

11/19/2020 #255

Day-159 "From the Heart"

From where do they come
A sweat soaked sheet
A night on the beach
Someone you cannot reach

Are they scenes or merely dreams
Silly songs or playful schemes
Loves that have gone wrong
Some that were really strong

An old man with a smile
A friend who told a lie

A monarch fluttering by
An eagle soaring high

An old, weathered door
What's hidden within its core

Have you ever wondered
From where they thundered

They are but art
From deep within your heart

These rhyming lines

11/21/2020 #256

Day-159 "Borrowed Paintings"

I took them for my own
Their colors divine
Their scenes sublime
Their brush strokes felt
From masters of their art

De Grazia in Tucson
Gavin in San Antonio
Picasso in the Ludwig
Mono Lisa in the Louvre

I took them for my own
Hung them on my wall
Indescribable beauty
From the masters of their art

They are but borrowed paintings
Treasures of my heart
Borrowed moments
Photos on my wall

For indeed I am a thief
Thank You Masters of your Art

11/21/2020 #257

Day-160 "Laying Planks"

So much endured
So many tears
It is but time
To lay four planks
Across this Valley
We call "Despair"

There is no guarantee
That life will ever be sane
Each triumph
Will always bring rain

The journey hard
The steps steep
The planks heavy
They'll leave blisters
On your hands
I'll guarantee

Lay the first
For the one you lost

Lay the second
For the disease that kills

Lay a third
For our people who
Do not matter

Lay a fourth
For the man who
Must bring peace

Do not relent
You must
Sharpen your blades
We need many more

This valley is wide
The river runs fast
Remember your mask
It's time to heal
And finish our task

11/22/2020 #258

Day-161 "My Undraped Lover"

Around your heart there shines a light
Illuminating the love hidden inside

Around your face there shines a light
Illuminating the smile that sits upon

Once painted by Michelangelo
Often scripted by Thoreau

The aura of your artistry
The beauty of your soul
Angelic your innocence
Purity your virginity

Your Halo I adore
Let me feast upon you more

        11/23/2020 #259

Day-162 "Halos"

There are thousands
In the midnight sky
God's Palace brightly shines
Aurora Borealis is its name

A crown of light
Radiates its face
October moon
In full bloom

Circles around a
Noon day sun
Growing fields
Will soon be blessed

A radiant face
Sharing life with
Little one at her breast

Angelic beauty
After love
Plants a flower
In her soul

Even on the cross
A "Halo" found his face

Serenity comes to mind
Purity surely rhymes
When "Halos" brighten
Our many days

        11/24/2020 #260

Day-165 "Creative Possibilities"

They are sometimes
More than we can grasp
Like Purity and Humility

They, sometimes
Vault and run
Like Calamity and Insanity

They, sometimes
Lead us astray
Like Pretentious and Infectious

They, sometimes
Come unwrapped
Like Precious and Sensuous

They, sometimes
Preach and Teach
Of Ill and Will

They, sometimes
Laugh at all the riffraff
On subway walls

And sometimes
They just want
To play a Cello in Acapella

What the Hell?

Sometimes I haven't a clue
What this is all about.
For they are no more
Than possibilities

11/27/2020 #261

Day-166 "Kindness"

What is it we've learned?
From those whom we're around
From the voices we've heard

What is it we've learned?
From the choices we've made
From the lovers we've loved

What is it we've learned?
From the lives we've made
From the joys we've had

What is it we've learned?
From secrets we've kept
From thoughts we've never said

What is it we've learned?
Kindness is a good word

11/28/2020 #262

Day-167 "An Affair"

I had an affair
I kept it a secret

Kept it hidden deep
Within my brain

It was sometimes unruly
Yet full of passion

It wasn't unkind
But it was blind

We shared many lines
And afternoon wines

We slipped behind locked doors
And sang in the choir

We had afternoon delights
And sometimes fights

We sat in parks
Until it was dark

We lit candles
And burned many a page

We wrote many a line
That didn't rhyme

Heaven forbid
If you thought it a sin.

It was but an affair
Just me and my pen

11/29/2020 #263

Day-168 "Don't be a Fool"

Dear: Cowboy on the Hill

It's time to pull on your boots
Cinch up old Nellie
And ride off into the sunset.

We're a gettin' mighty tired
The people have spoken

From: A cowboy from the west

11/30/220 #264

Day 168 "Enchanted Forest"

Ten thousand came knocking
Knocking at a forest door

They heard of strange delights
And wizardry found therein

They came to unravel
The mysteries hidden within

From within was heard
A booming voice

Who's that knocking
On my forest door?

Tis us
The ten thousand proclaimed

We demand to know what's hidden inside
Let us search the bowels of your forest
For the witchcraft and mysteries therein

To which the voice replied
There are no mysteries hidden within
Just bark and boughs and forest lives
That nip at you in midnight dreams

Your demands cannot be met
Your entry I will not let

The ten thousand
Ranted and raved
Stewed and screamed
      Then
Grabbed a bar and pried the door
And in they streamed
To a forest lush and green
Birds singing in the trees
Deer grazing in the vales

Upon a hill
An old man stood
A tablet in his hand

Would you be so kind
As not to disturb my mind
Your actions I cannot condone
You are free to gaze about
But then you must leave
This beauty I will share
Only for a moment

With that he closed his tablet
Lightning stuck and thunder boomed
Hail rained down on the ten thousand
Not a leaf was harmed nor a creature disturbed
As out the ten thousand ran

At the door, a maiden stood giving each a scroll
Upon which was writ
This is my time
This is my rhyme
Come again when you can be kind

11/30/2020 #265

This is about a poet trying to write a poem while being distracted and surrounded by people wanting to know what is inside his mind.

Day-170 "Inspiration"

Where oh where have you gone?
Are you lost?
Can't find your way home

Did you discover
Then forget
What you discovered?

There is no denying
You can get lost
It's not a crime

Damn good thing you're
Not a soldier
Trapped behind enemy lines

Damn good thing you're
Not an astronaut
Lost in a galaxy far away

Damn good thing you're
Not a snowman
Melting away in Panama

How about a sailor lost at sea
A mermaid who cannot swim
A cowboy without a horse

There's something to being lost
A hidden emotion
An empty emotion
It's like where did my brain go.

Is that it sitting on my garden wall?
We all get lost every once in a while

12/2/2020 #266

Day-170 "Simple Pleasures"

They came fluttering and flittering
Dancing and twirling
First one here, then one there
A sight to behold
As they searched for gold
Surveying the flowers
With radar beams
The scent of the nectar
Drawing them near
A purple one they chose

Upon which they sat
Their orange and black wings
Came to rest
And they began to feast

All for my pleasure
On this sunny day
I would surely share

Bring a glass of Chablis
And sit awhile with me

12/2/2020 #267

Day-170 "Sit, Sat and Set"

Sit and sat
Set on a wall
Along came set
And sat between
Sit and sat
To which sat said
Move your ass over
You silly sit

12/02/2020 #268

Day-170 "Sit, Sat and Set-2"

Sit and sat
Set on a wall
Sit and sat
Had a great fall
All the Kings horses
And
All the Kings men
Couldn't put
Sit and sat back together
 Again

Poor ol' set
Was never the
Same

12/02/2020 #269

So much for the tales of sit, sat and set..... Sometimes we all need to be a little silly. My wife is always correcting my sits and sets, as I never get them right. It seems I'm always looking for a seat.

Day-171 "Situations"

I locked myself out
I broke the glass
It cost me a grand

I awoke at ten
She was gone
Her slip on the floor
Who was she, I asked

Two little boys
Playing in a tree
One fell down
The other came
And pulled him back up

You say you won
I say you lost
Let's put on gloves
Then go have a beer

So happy you came
Lobster for two
A bottle of chardonnay
Would you mind
I haven't a dime

A man in blue
Came knocking at my door
Sign here monsieur
You must appear

I touched her once
She thought it a pass
And kicked me in the ass
I thought we were friends

I laughed at his joke
But it wasn't kind
I should've walked away
He was more important than I

There are many a day
Each moment is one
You have to choose
The paint you will use

12/03/2020 #270

Day-171 "No Regrets"

We sculpted angels in the snow
Chased rainbows when it rained
Molded castles in the sand
Walked in deserts before the noon day sun
Took our chances when we were young

We sailed off cliffs in Acapulco
Made love on the isle of Capri
Sipped wine in Monterey
Took our chances when we were young

Sometimes we cried
Sometimes we sighed
Sometimes we tried
Sometimes we took it all in stride
We took our chances when we were young
Following our love around the world

12/03/2020 #271

Day-173 "Things"

Friends:
Everyone should have one
There're like pets
You know, like cats and dogs
Maybe a monkey for whenever
You're down and out

Lovers:
Someone to keep you warm
Take walks within evening hours
Talk to whenever you're blue
Or when you don't have
Anything else to do

Adventures:
They open you up
To many new things,
Like places and dreams
Secrets and themes
Doors that are green

Obsessions:
They're like an itch
That won't dissipate
Flying down a hill
At one hundred and eight

Impulses:
Kiss her now
Before you part
Sometimes it works
Sometimes they run away

Art:
Paint it bright
Sing it loud
Write it right
It tells the times
Expands the mind

Sometimes it isn't what it is.
But then it is

          12/05/2020 #272

Day-174 "Curiosity"

What's beyond what we see?
A sailboat on an ocean blue
A trail that has no end
A forest full of trees
A view from forty-five up
Have you ever wondered what?
What's beyond what we see?
A man without a coat
A home without a bed
A child without a home
A woman without love
Have you ever wondered why?

What's beyond what we see?
A morning without dew
A sky without a cloud
A sunset that no one sees
A night without a star
Have you ever wondered why?

What's beyond what we see?
A roomful of laughter
A puppy chasing a ball
A seaside romp

A walk in a park
Have you ever wondered what?
Have you ever wandered beyond?

12/06/2020 #273

Day-174 "Wanderings"

They come in scenes and
Dreams without themes
Memories and schemes
Of lovers that did not love

They attack at Two AM
Wander around till
Sunlight beams
And meadowlarks sing

They're found on lonely highways
In midnight hours
Roads that have no end

In fields a farmer and a plough
Back and forth
Days that do not end

A woman writing lines
That do not rhyme
Is not a waste of time

Haven't your thoughts
Ever wandered beyond
Running free without a pen?

12/06/2020 #274

Day-174 "The Poet's Fare"

Penning life differently
Is the poet's fare
Selling metaphors
For his love affairs

Penning lines
That sing in harmony
Painting shadows
With a pen

Rafting rivers
That do not cry
Exploring mountains
That have no names

Molten lightning
On a desert plane
Thunder in the morning rain
Searching for gold
At rainbow's end
Laughter in every line

Soldier looking for love
On red lit street
Dark and lonely is the night

Master of the Metaphor
There are yet many more
For the poet who pays the fare

12/06/2020 #275

Day-175 "Transcendence"

Cross over, cross over
Oh, knight in black cape

Let us partake
The fruits of your mind
Speak to us in words that rhyme
Tell us tales of love and crime

Become one like us
We're easy to please
Hasten your pace
Let us embrace

Cast off your cape
Set yourself free
Let your soul bleed
There is great need

We are but brothers
Cross over cross over

12/07/2020 #276

In a spiritual sense this poem is about changing your attitude toward those of a different color, nationality, religion or sexual orientation.

It is about sharing your lives, telling your stories, overcoming your prejudices. In other words, it's about getting your mind to accept those different than you.

Day-177 "Summer's Past"

Faded Thoughts
Are all I have left
Of the love we chased
The laughter we shared
Playing on that shore
In the spring of our lives

We gave it a chance
Knowing it wouldn't last
Knowing we had to pass

I return every once in a while
To this shore beside the sea
It replenishes my inner soul
The sounds and scents of the sea
Sandpipers to and fro
Castles in the sand

A lovely collection
Brings to mind
Of a wonderful time
The sounds and scents of the sea
Your wet body clinging to mine

12/09/2020 #277

Day-180 "Prescriptions"

Old Doc Master
Was a master crafter
Whatever you were after
He made it with laughter

He took a pinch of this
And a tickle of that
Mixed it up in a porcelain bowl
Was sure to cure anything
That ailed your poor soul
Guaranteed to make you whole

One day I said I was ill
I was down and dumpy
I had no will

He took my temp
Then said with a thrill
What you need is a pinch of song

From the shelf he pulled and old 32
And gave it a spin
Out of that old horn came
The most beautiful melody
I have ever heard
Sung by a lady in a pink polka dot thong

Wow! Was all I could muster
I can't remember the song
But I do the thong.
As I laughed all the way home

On another occasion
I was quite blue
I asked old Doc Master
What I should do

Without a word
He pulled from the shelf
A leather-bound book
The title of which was
"Poems for the Soul"
He opened it to page 32
Thereupon which was writ

I want to be a rock star
On the moon
Sing songs with the galaxies
In my yellow submarine
Take a rocket ship to Mars
On Sunday after church

He said with a grin
In order to chase the blues
You gotta take clues
Drink a little gin
As you play your violin

I laughed all the way home

It was a Saturday night
And I was not gay
I spied old Doc in a lusty old bar
Surrounded by gorgeous delights
Having the time of his life

What ails you, my son?
It appears, without a doubt
That you are down and out.
Is there something I can do for you?

You helped me when I was ill
And you gave me a girl singing a song
In a polka dot thong
And I sang all the way home
You helped me when I was blue

You read me an un-rhyming rhyme
And I rhymed it all the way home

Now I am sad and in need of joy
What is it you have that will make me joyfully fun?

To which he replied.
Have you tried dancing?

With that he jumped up and clicked his heels,
Grabbed one of the delightfuls and
Swirled her about the room

See, it's not as hard as you think
You just gotta let go.

Thereupon I grab a delightful
And delightfully danced
All the way home

12/11/2020 #278

Day-181 "The Prairie"

As far as the eye can see
The mind stands still

So vast there is no end
How small we are

Where buffalo once roamed
And antelope played

Where meadowlarks sing
On yucca plant stems

Where raptors circle
In the blue above

Where the wind
Whispers through the grass

Where sunsets
Paint the western skies

Where coyotes howl
On moon lit nights

Where brighter stars
Won't ever be found

Where ancient men
Once did hunt

Ten thousand years
Have come and gone

Out here the prairie
Is much the same

That first taste of the prairie
The vastness of it all
Belittles the mind
How small we are

So many
Oh, so many
Live in divided walls
In concrete towers
Searching for places
To sooth their souls

Go!

Go find a prairie
Listen to the wind

As it whispers
Through the grass

Where meadowlarks sing
Prairie melodies
In early dawns

12/12/2020) #279

On one of my many journeys across western Kansas I came upon this landmark of a place in Logan County, Kansas. It is named the "Little Jerusalem Badland State Park". It was a project of the Nature Conservancy and the State of Kansas. Much to my delight I stopped and walked about the park for the better part of the morning. The wind was chilly, out of the south, causing the grass to sway in rhythm to its ebb and flow. It was just a typical Kansas morning on the western Kansas plains. It is with great gratitude and appreciation to the "Nature Conservancy" for preserving sights like this for all to enjoy.

Day-182 "Desert Morning"

Early morning light
Sun yet to breach
Mountain of the east

Nature's music rings
Crisp and clear

Mother Earth in bloom
Her perfume fills the air
How little time we have

Good Morning, we say
To unknown passers by

To be so blessed
Tis life at its best
How little time we have

                                        12/12/2020 #280

Photo of sunrise near, Tucson, AZ

Day-183 "Smiles"

What puts a smile on your face?
A rose
A butterfly
A rainbow
The beauty of being at peace with nature
Roses, Butterflies and Rainbows

What puts a smile on your face?
Someone you've loved
Someone you've helped
Someone you've taught
The beauty of being at peace with your heart
Loving, Helping and Teaching

What puts a smile on your face?
Being kind
Being grateful
Being truthful
The beauty of being at peace with your soul
Compassion, Charity and Honesty

Smiles bring beauty beyond compare
They open many a door
Try putting a
Smile upon your face
They open many a door

12/13/2020 #281

Day-184 "Reformation-2"

I sang a Song
A long time ago
It was full of sadness
Lost loves and old cowboys
It made me cry

I then saw a man
With a fiddle and a flute
Playing reggae in a dark leather suite
I sing no more of
Lost loves and old cowboys

                                                  12/14/2020 #282

Day-184 "A Mountain Melody"

Your majesty
In snow white crown
High above the plains you rise

I knelt and prayed that someday
I would own you for my own
America! America!
Shed some grace on thee

I will bring you jewels
From the plains
Dress your throne in velvet blue
America! America!
Shed some grace on thee

A masterpiece
A patriot's theme
A pilgrim's dream
"America the Beautiful"
Shed some grace on thee

Sing it loud
Sing it proud
Tis our country
Tis of thee
America! America!
Shed some grace on thee

Till nobler men once again
Shine their lights on thee

12/14/2020 #283

I currently live near the noble mountain called Pikes Peak. It is indeed America's Mountain. When it snows on the peak it brings to mind all the wonderful things we have and can share with the rest of the world, even in times of turmoil. Katharine Bates Wrote the poem "Pikes Peak" in 1893. It is truly a wonderful poem. The most popular melody was written by Samuel A Ward. "America the Beautiful" published in 1910.

Day-186 "Reformation-3"

I wrote a story
A long time ago
About two lovers
Who fought and stole apart
I felt sorry for the two

One night in New York
I saw two lovers dancing
Across the square
They kissed and held each other tight
I wrote no more of lovers that quarrel

12/16/2020 #284

Day 187 "Times Square @ Three AM"

It was Three AM
The night air cold
As scenes began to unfold
Each worth a thousand rhyming lines

I watched them dance
Across the square
Stop and kiss
Then move on

It was 1945 all over again
I took it all in

                                                12/17/2020 #285

Day 187 "Times Square @ Three AM, Dancers"

On a ledge across the way
Young men spied my hidden spot
Jumped up and began to dance
I was enthralled to say the least
They were dancers of the dark

I felt safe that night
Alone on the street
People like me
Wanting to be
Watching the scenes
Times Square at Three AM

12/17/2020 #286

Day-189 "This Hallowed Eve"

Sing your carols
Sing them loud
Let them ring
Throughout the land

How a pauper's son came to pass
Reminders of the past

How a baby in a manger
Simple as that is

How a night turned silent
How a star shown bright

From a pauper to a king
How this moment came to pass
How great is that?

How a simple moment
Changed the world

Sing praise to him this eve
For the presents he bestowed
On all mankind

Sing your carols
Loud and clear
For the king who came
This hallowed eve.

12/19/2020 #287

Day-189 "Christmas Eve Cowgirl"

The candles lit

The bread taken

Her lips wetted

Lady with

Little boots by her side

Crosses her heart

Says a pray

For her cowboy

Out fixing fence and breaking ice.

                                                12/19/2020) #288

Day-189 "Old Cowboys and Cowgirls"

Old cowboys never die
They just
Saddle up and drift away

Cowgirls never cry
They just cinch up their cowboys
And ride em till they're glassy eyed

                                                12/19/2020 #289

Day-190   "Reality Checks"

It's not who you were
It's who you are

Its's not what you used to do
It's what you do

Its's not what you want to be
It's who you are

It's not where you are from
It's where you are

It's not about the pace
It's the journey you're on

It's not about where you are going
It's what you learn along the way

Will you be happy and gay?
Will you find peace along the way?

Step back and take a look
Each step you take
Requires a reality check

                         12/20/2020 #290

Day-191 "Manhood"

What is it?
Standing up
To life's challenges

What is it?
Taking your lumps
When things go wrong

What is it?
Pulling yourself up
When you fall

What is it?
Giving in
When there is no end

What is it?
Recognizing reality
When you are proved wrong

What is it?
Admitting you lost
When you didn't win

What is it?
Some call it courage
Some call it being a man
I call it manhood.

                                              12/21/2020 #291

313Day-191 "Reality Checks II"

A question for the red cappers

Would you deny the simple fact that the 49's lost the "Super Bowl" 31-20 to the Chiefs in 2020?
Would you ask the Supreme Court to overturn the score?
Would you ask the NFL to toss out the 4th Quarter?
Would you hire Rudy G. to defend your claim?

Really?

        You would?

  You just gotta laugh at that
                                      12/21/2020 #292

Day-191 "Jerry Lee"

You da Man
Jerry Lee
You and your Pink Cadillac
Play it loud
Play it
All night long

We goanna dance across
That Walmart parking lot
Till we all fall down
And the morning sun
Strokes our brains
                                      12/21/2020 #293

Play Jerry Lee Lewis's "Last Man Standing" CD and you'll get the drift

Day-193 "Very Bad Santa Crawl"

Once upon a time
I wandered upon this scene
Was quite a jolly bunch
Down in New Orleans

Down on Bourbon Street
Where bad boys and girls come to play
Some say it's for charity
Some say it's for fun
I say it looks like they all
Just wanna get drunk

What would Santa think
If he really knew
What was in that brew?

Whoa there Rudolph!
Looks like fun's about to take place
The children will have to wait
Cause I'm gonna be late

Octane for two Please
Poor ol' Rudolph
Needs a little more juice
He's up on the roof top
Stealing a feel and
Stomping his feet

Out of the Bijous
They stumbled
An army of Santas
All dressed in red
Drums and trumpets
Tambourines and cowbells
Crashing the scene
Without a theme
If you know what I mean

Poor ol' Santa
His hair all a mess
Lipstick on his beard
His cap borrowed for a kiss
Fell flat on his face

Up on the roof top
Rudolph was all a miss
His nose all shiny
His antlers aflame
Cried out to the crowd
Bring Ol' Santa back
We have places to be

With a jug in his hand
And a silly eating grin
Ol' Santa crawled back
To his sleigh and with a grand
       "Hi Ho"
Off the roof top they flew

Now all you mothers and fathers out there,
Never tell this story to your little ones
For they will wonder where you've been
When you come home stinking of gin
Before Christmas Eve ends.

For there ain't no place like
Bourbon Street when
Santa comes to town

Yaw Hoo! Bring on the cheer

          12/23/2020 #294

Day-196 "Good Riddance"

Put some blue sky in my day
Put a smile on my face
It's time to rejoice
2020 is fading away.

          12/26/2020 #295

Day-196 "A Poetic Love Affair"

It may come as no surprise
To artists of the written word
That when you discover
A poet you really love
You want to marry their words

So was the case this day
When I discovered
Georgia Douglas Johnson
So simple yet powerful
Her poetic words
A lasting love affair with my soul

12/26/2020 #296

Georgia Douglas Johnson 1880-1966

Day-196 "Voyage"

This journey dark and cold
Seeks to break us of our mold

Many mountains yet to climb
As we seek mysterious rhymes

Some say happiness we will find
Others say it will make us blind

What is better I must ask
Am I but a vagrant ass?

Searching for gold in trying times
For peeling back layers of mystic lines

For its joy that I seek
And laughter for the meek

I too wish this journey to end
And we no longer have to fend

The heavens will surely open
And joy will reign once again.

                                                   12/26/2020 #297

Day-196 "Caged"

Let's Tango in Grand Parie
Jitter in old Hamburg

Sing songs in Japanese
Sail the ocean on a breeze

Ride a horse to Tim Buck Too
Visit your uncle at the zoo

Take a photo with the Pope
He will surely give us hope

Oh, the fun we'll have
When they let us out of here

                                                   12/26/2020 #298

Day-197 "I Am a Simple Man"

Please
Don't tell me secrets
I care not to understand

Don't fill my brain
With sanctimonious thoughts
That tie me in knots

I am but a simple man
Not hard to understand

Speak not of gossip
I am not your mailman
I have no plan

I'll cherish your thoughts of love
Even though I am unworthy of

I'll awaken you with a kiss
And love you in the evening mist

I am but a simple man
Not hard to understand

I'll bring you tidings of good will
Even when you are ill

I can't change the course of history
It's too complicated for my brain

But I can tell you stories
That will make you kind
And laugh at the same time

I am but a simple man
Not hard to understand   12/27/2020 #299

Day-197 "Smilestone-300"

The mystery to be solved
By seekers at the gate
Telling us tales of woe
Of courage, fortitude and triumph
Tales of disappointment and sorrow
Kindness and gratitude
Laughter and joy

The many planks that it takes
To finish the bridge that spans
The "Valley of Despair"
through which a raging river flows.

Today marks the three hundredth poem in my quest to write Three hundred and sixty-five, positive, feel good poems.

                                                                          12/27/2020 #300

Day-200 "Beauty"

I wanted to write about beauty today
When I discovered
All I had to do was
Look around

I wanted to write about joy today
When I discovered
All I had to do was
Change the script

I wanted to write about love today
When I discovered
All I had to do was
Say how much I loved her

I wanted to write about hope today
When I discovered
All I had to do was
Go to church and pray

I wanted to write about kindness today
When I discovered
All I had to do was
Open a door for a lady friend

I wanted to write about gratitude today
When I discovered
All I had to do was
Write a note to a friend

I wanted to write a million lines today
When I discovered
All I had to do was
"Look Around"

12/30/2020 # 301

Day-201 "December Glow"

Oh, beautiful moon glow night
Save me from the fright
That begs my soul to write

Let me savor your glow
Reflections on the snow
Stitched in my brain for ever more

                                        12/31/2020 #302

Day-201 "Lost Dreams"

I'm having dreams
About lost scenes
That have no themes
Or so it seems

Roust out your sadness
Vanquish your blackness
Bring on your gladness

New days are dawning
Reclaim your calling
No time for stalling

Prepare your arms
Sound the alarm
Pour on the charm

There's no time to doubt
There's no time to pout
Let your voices shout out

Bring it on I say
Soak my head in laughter
You nighttime crafters
Rain it from the rafters
Merry thoughts forever after

                                              12/31/2020 #303

Day-201 "Change the Script"

Tis time to change the script.
And write anew
Of things we know
But cannot change

Take sadness, gloom and doom
And throw them in a cell
Let them soak in solitary
Forever and a day

Set you pens to happiness, joy and fun
Let them sing across this land
Let them bask in sunshine
Forever and a day
Tis time to change the script

                                                12/31/2020 #304

Day-201 "So Proud"

So proud was he
Our little weasel friend
As he scampered past
Our window glass

Pausing for a moment
To show his catch
For his New Year's feast

You've done well
My little friend
We're so proud of you
We wish you well this joyous day

My sympathy for the mouse
That didn't get away.

12/31/2020 #305

Day-201 "Hey Days"

An old farmer once said
You make hay when the sun shines bright
And lay in the shade when it's not right

Plant your seeds in May
And you will never be dismayed

Till a straight line
And it will make you fine

If it rains on your parade
Don't become frayed

An old poet once said
Put a rhyme in your pocket
Turn it into a sonnet

Pen a poem in morning light
Sing with it till twilight flights

Never chase the moment
High is the cost of atonement
When time is ripe
Waste not your type.

Don't lay in the shade
When it's time to make your hey

         12/31/2020 #306

Day-201 "Good Riddance 2020"

I'm wearing black today
There is a funeral I must attend
It's for my friend
"Good old 2020"

I'm wearing black today
Am wearing it with pride
For there is "Joy" inside
Good old 2020 has passed away

Never more shall I mourn
For good old 2020
Was more than I could stand

So, I wear black today
For the "Joy" it brings
And the smile that grows
Upon my face

Come 11:59 I'll tear it from my back
Raise my glass and grasp
My rusty spade and
Bury Good old 2020 six feet down.
I'm wearing black today

   "Good Riddance 2020"
           12/31/2020 #307

Day-202 "Decisions"

I decided not to rehash it
Not to go back and fight it
It's not something
I want anymore

I decided not to write of it
Not to spoil my ink
They are just words
I care not to write

I decided not to think about it
Not to burn space in my brain
They are just thoughts
That have no results

I decided not to dream of it
For it was a fantasy
That would not come true

      So

When I'm done rehashing
When I'm done writing
When I'm done thinking
And when I'm done dreaming of her

I'll be free
To sit under my tree
Whistling a tune that no one hears
And laugh at the squirrel who can't find his nuts

1/01/2021 #308

Day-205 "Sunshine"

Sunshine on the mountain
Brings a smile to my face

Sunshine over the ocean waves
Brings teardrops to my eyes

Sunshine setting over distant plain
Brings me peace of mind

Sunshine after a morning rain
Puts a rainbow in my soul

Sunshine on your face
Begs me to love you more.

1/03/2021 #309

Day-205 "That Song"

(An ode to John Denver)

If I had a day
I would fill it with sunshine
And stroll along an ocean shore

If I could name a day
I would name it "Sunshine"
And never name another day

If I could sing a song
I would sing about sunshine
And John who gave us that song

1/03/2021 #310

Day-209 "Help"

Today, I thought about hate
How it burns my soul

I thought about hope
How it brightens my soul

I thought about love
How it fulfills my soul

I thought about friendships
How blessed they are

I then thought about help
How I needed it
To overcome my hate
To brighten my soul
To share my love
To be thankful for my friends

1/07/2021 #311

Day-209 "Decoding"

Poets write sad poems
Because they are sad

They write about love
Because they desire it

They write about joy
Because they need it

They write about beauty
Because they see it

They write about affairs
Sunsets and moon glows

They write about many a thing
In metaphoric lines
Unraveling puzzles hidden
Deep in their minds

                        1/07/2021 #312

Day-210 "Ode to Old "Dink"

I once had a horse
That most would call a disgrace
For he had the ugliest head
You ever did see
But boy could he walk
He was the fastest by far
I loved that old horse
As ugly as he was
You'd thought him a mule

He was gangly and lean
Part strawberry roan
Eighteen hands high
A tail that reached to the ground
A head almost as long and
Stocking feet that didn't match

But it didn't seem to bother ol' "Dink"
With a "giddy up"
And a touch of a spur
He'd be long gone
Along with your hat
If it wasn't tied down.

It was one day, about six o'clock sun
ol'"Dink" and I rode out the gate
Cattle to check over distant plain

About ten miles gone
When out of the prairie
An old rattler *Hissssed*
Took a snip at ol' "Dink"
And up he reared
And out of the saddle I flew

It wasn't the softest of landings
As I recall. A broken rib
A leg shattered in two.

Well, ol'"Dink", he stood there
For a minute or two
Wondering what he should do
When all of a sudden up on his
Hind legs he reared
His hoofs cursed the sky and
With a mighty downward thrust
Severed the head of that pesky old snake

Well as best as I could I skinned
That old rattler right there and then

Thereupon ol' "Dink"
Got down on his knees and
With a nod of his head
Pushed me astride him again
And back to the ranch house we flew

It's been many a year since I was ten
I remember well those hot summer days
And counting dad's cows
Bullet hawks circling above
Diving at locusts flushed from the sage
Dad waiting at the barn

Did you get the count right son?

As always ol' "Dink" was my best friend for
He saved me from many a frightful scene
It seemed he just loved that silver bridle
Its rattle snake headband and me on his back

1/08/2021 #313

Day-211 "A Simple Kiss"

There's a weed in my back yard
It's tall and lanky
It's black, mean and ugly

I've chopped it down
three times today
each time I turn
it flares up again and again

As I was scratching my head
wondering what to do
along came a little boy
with a candy cane smile

Howdy Mr. Smith!
I see you've been
working hard today
just what is it you are trying to do?

I'm trying to rid my yard
of this pesky ol' weed
I've chopped it down
three times today
each time I turn
it flares up again and again

With a twinkle in his eye
and a grin on his face
the little boy said.
I betcha I can rid
it from your yard?
Would you let me give it a try?

Sure, I said
If you do, I'll give you a smile

With that the little boy
with the candy cane smile
ran to my back yard and
planted a kiss on that ugly ol' weed

To my utter amazement
it wilted and died
right there on the spot

My Goodness! Said I
How on earth did you do that?
What is this magic you possess?

Where upon the little boy
with the candy cane smile
Said,

You kill hate with kindness
Mr. Smith
Now, may I have my smile?

>   1/09/2021#314

Day-212 "Rainbows"

A smile graces my face
Whenever a rainbow
Discovers my space

>   1/10/2021 #315

Day-212 "Journeys"

I wrote a poem
And set it loose
Across the plains

I sang a song
And let it sail
Across the ocean waves

I played at love
And let it climb
Above the snowcapped peaks

Please pray these are
But a few
Of the many
Yet to be

                                          1/10/2021 #316

Day-213 "Lightning"

I could see the lightning
Illuminating the sky
Sharp Cracks
Poisoned arrows
Striking the earth
In unknown vales

I had to let her go.
I could see the lightning
But never felt the thunder

                                          1/11/2021 #317

Day-213 "Second Thoughts"

Jolting upright
A bolt of lightning
Struck my heart
Freezing veins deep inside
I was wrong
She was right
I ran to catch her
When darkness struck

                                                1/11/2021 #318

Day-215 "Opportune"

Ride that wave when it comes
Climb that mountain in the dawn
Kiss the sun as it falls
Spill some ink upon a page
Never let a day go by
Without a cherished high

                                                1/13/2021 #319

Day-215 "Flower Garden"

She wove Tulips
In her hair
Sunflowers in her eyes
Roses on her cheeks
And Daisies in her smile

The love of my life
A garden blooming
In my
Four poster bed

                                                1/13/2021 #320

Day-217 "Inspired"

She spoke of Joy, Peace and Harmony
She led me in
And locked the door

I fell in Love
Now here we lie
No longer do I cry

                                          1/15/2021 #321

Day-217 "Satisfaction"

He scaled a steep hill
And gazed across the plain

She wrote a beautiful line
Then put it aside

He stood awhile
She smiled within

                                            1/15/2021 #322

Day-217 "AWESOME"

There are many things to
Wonder at

But none so beautiful

As blooming suns
Over eastern plains

And fading rays
Over ocean waves

                                          1/15/2021 #323

Day-217 "Gratitude"

I have a beautiful wife
Who knows how to please
Children who have not sinned
A place to rest my bones
An empty page
And a pen full of ink

                              1/15/2021 #324

Day-219 "Happiness"

Oh, you ancient men
Travelers searching
Across the plains

Seekers looking
For a treasure
Never finding
Always chasing

Thought they found
It once upon
Even held it in their palm
Yet it escaped in the dawn

Fleeting moments
Never understood
Never in their minds
What they couldn't own

Oh, ye seekers....

Have you never looked around
It's with you all the time
No need to mount that crest
Nor turn that stone
It only hides within your mind
Tis a choice you make
Each and every time

                                                      1/17/2021 #325

Day-223 "I Am Your Constitution"

In the wee hours of the night
There came a pounding on my door
Up from my bed I rose

Who's that pounding on my door?
Why are you pounding on my door?

Wake up! Wake up!
It's raining hard outside
And I, not a cover for my head

Let me in! Let me in!
Lightning bolts are searing the sky
Thunder's fury is raging mad
Tears are falling from my eyes

Who's that pounding on my door?
Why are you pounding on my door?

In night cloth bare
I stumbled to the door
Only to find a silhouette
Running circles in my brain
And back to bed I cowered

In my deep night slumber
I heard a rapping at my door
Up from my bed I rose

Who's that rapping at my door?
Why are you rapping at my door?
Surely tis not another dream

I heard a mournful whisper
Let me in, Let me in
Men are coming! Men are coming!
I need shelter from their swords
Let me in, Let me in

Again, I stumbled to the door
And peered upon a ghostly scene
Was surely not a dream
Marching in midnight mist
Ten thousand men had gathered steam
Marching to my door

I heard a mournful whisper
From somewhere high
Whereupon I spied an Eagle perched
An "Olive Branch"
Clenched in his beak

Again, I heard that mournful whisper
Let me in!   Let me in!
Men are coming to take this branch
Help me please, or I will die
Ten thousand men are gathering steam
An insurrection coming to your steep

With that I flung wide the door
And in the Eagle flew
And settled on the mantle
Above the warming coals

I bolted the door
And closed the shutters
As they pounded and cursed
Unleashing their steam

A window was breeched
The Eagle Screamed
An ungodly screech
And to the glass he flew
Beating back the ten thousand
With his olive branch

And I, the book held high
Began to read to those inside and out
And all who began to doubt

"WE THE PEOPLE of the United States
In order to form a more perfect union"
....

There was much blood
On our steps that day
But I and the Eagle
Pushed back and broke their backs

As I recall those powerful words
Written in blood by many of our kind
And etched in our souls for immortal time
I am reminded of how powerful
I really am and the podium on which I lie

For all the men and women of these United States
This is the book on which **"United"** we stand.
The oath some take to lead us through
Many a trying time.

1/21/2021 #326

Day-224 "Together We Stand"

We stand bruised and battered
Our resolve still strong
To heal the sick
Repair our hearts
Take back our pride

We are but soldiers of peace
A battalion of faith
An army of hope
A nation of proud people

Upon this high ground
We stand once more
A shining light
A beacon in the night

We've chosen to live
With compassion in our souls
And love in our hearts
For all mankind

Let this army of Hope
Lead us forever on
With justice and peace
For all our people

Together we stand
A new day has dawned

                        1/22/2021 #327

Day-228 "Hope Crystals"

From out of the dark
In the darkest of the darkest night
In the darkest of the darkest day
There came a man in tattered cloth
About his waist a simple rope
And leather pouch

To all he passed he gifted a gem
Each in-scripted with a rhyme
A tiny crystal with a theme

To a mother with child, he reached inside
And pulled out Lepidolite.
Upon which was writ
Hold me tight in the middle
Of the night.
The sun will shine
In the morning light
This is my gem I gift to you

To a little boy
Fishing by a stream
He pulled out "Aventurine"
Was of aqua green
Here, put this in your pocket
And mind you never hock it
"When you are feeling ugly
Remember how lucky
You really are"

There was a little girl
Swinging from a branch
The higher she swung the more she squealed
Her name was Gemonite
To her he gifted "Alexandrite"
On which he wrote

Put joy in your locket and
Swing high like a bird in the sky
Let it rain laughter to all who pass you by

He passed a farmer in a field
Plowing and planting seeds
His wife in their kitchen
Canning their many needs
From his pouch he pulled
A light green gem called "Peridot"
And placed it in the farmer's hand
Bless these fields for
There is much to gain
From the sunshine and the rain

To a poet
In a dream like state
He shared a "Sunstone"
When your words are right
Tell us of what you write
There are many sonnets
Hidden in your soul

To two young lovers
Exchanging vows
In white steepled church
He bestowed a "Rose Quartz"
Open your hearts
For they dissolve old hurts
Put your trust in love
There are many stanzas
In the concerts of your lives.

He paused by
A man without labor
A family to feed
Into his palm he placed
A crystal of "Snowflake Obsidian"
Cherish this gem

Is but an envelope
To hold your dreams
A star soon to sew
Onto your Royal Diadem

To a teacher
In front of her class
He laid a volume of "Sunstones"
For the dreams she caresses
Of her students who
Will learn to fly as high
As that bird up in the sky

He came upon
An army of soldiers
All battered and bruised
Dancing in the street
He laid before them a
A tin of "Spinel"
Around and around they danced
In the evening light
Spinel! Spinel! They shouted
Home from the fight
Is a joyous delight

A last he came upon
A man with pen and pad
Writing of what he had seen
From his pouch he pulled "Amazonite"
So all would know
As we should know
The blood that's let for truth

At the end of the darkest of the darkest night
And the darkest of the darkest day
The old man stopped
And spoke to the crowd gathered there.

Some say there is more
Some say there is some in every soul
But ten is enough

I leave you with this one called "Tiger Eye"
I found it in DC
Tis called the "Stone of Hope"
Look deep in his soul
And you will see the Hope
For all that be.

Statue of Martin Luther King. It is called the "Stone of Hope"

1/26/2021 #328

Day-228 "Rendezvous"

In the calm
Of early morning dawn
Ten thousand men came marching on
Ten thousand women clinging on
They sought a rendezvous

Blazing fires light the sky
Nightmares flying high
Buzzards slicing up the pie
Do we live or do we die
Dare we rendezvous?

A river deep and wide
Raging torrents rushing by
Questions we must answer why
This odyssey we must survive
Allow us please the other side
We must rendezvous

The horizon reaches out
Beckoning without doubt
The trials endured have been about
But we have a rendezvous
We have a rendezvous with Hope

                        1/26/2021 #329

Day-231 "Running Wild"

I'm running wild
Wild as a northern breeze

A cheetah on an African plain
A wolf in Idaho Springs

Inside me a calling
Calling to be free

Waves crashing the shores of my soul
Winds battering the doors of my being

Yield me a canvas
On which to paint

An ocean to sail
I'm running wild

Inside me a calling
Calling to be free

I need a mountain to climb
When I have nothing to do

A lover to undress
In the dark of the night

A river to forge
When my mind's not right

A friend to hold
When I am blue

Inside me a calling
Calling to be free
I'm running wild
Wild as a northern breeze

                              1/29/2021 #330

Day-234 "Revolution"

Open the doors
To your pine covered floors

Tear down the shutters
That's kept out the cold

Breath in the freshness
The south winds bring

Cast off your grays
New days are near

Embellish your cloth
With yellows and greens

Dust your silver
And set a fresh plate

Demand we all rise
When she arrives

A revolution is near
Stand up and sing praise

There is great charm
In new spring days

As winter's long days
Await cherry tree blossoms

2/01/2021 #331

This poem is not only about the springtime of the year but giving us hope that a new day will come once we are vaccinated against the COVID 19 virus.

Day-235 "It's Infectious"

A little boy came a running by
And I wondered why
Why he could be so jolly and gay
So, I asked him why

A little girl came a skipping by
And I wondered why
Why she could be so happy and free
So, I asked her why

An old man came a whistling by
And I wondered why
Why he could be so content and calm
So, I asked him why

A little puppy came a wandering up
And kissed my toes
His tail a wiggling and a waggling
And I began to smile

And then I knew why

The little boy said
I just love to run

And the little girl said
> *I just love to skip*

And the old man said
> *It's the only day I have*

And the puppy yipped'
> *And wagged his tail*

2/02/2021 #332

Day-236 "Vagrant Thoughts"

Have you ever wondered why
The sun comes up in the east
And never in the west?

Or why the moon never shines
On cloudy nights.

Why the Earth is round
And not flat

Why some are happy
And others not

Why some live
And others don't

Why you have a life
And I don't

Well, I have
And I'm sure
Many grave diggers
Have thought these thoughts as well

Have you ever wondered who
Designed it this way?

Or why great thoughts
Never come my way

Well, I have
And, Oh by the way
Would you mind
Passing that joint

2/03/2021 #333

Day-238 "Cosmic Relationships"

I read his poem
I crawled around inside
The caverns of his mind
Thinking I was one with him
His words came out
As if they were my own

Your sayings I know are true
I desire to be much more like you

2/5/2021 #334

Day-238 "Sequel to Cosmic Relationships"

I read a poem
I crawled around inside
The caverns of its mind
Thinking I was one with it
The words came out
As if they were my own

The script I know is true
The moment I know is "Now"

2/5/2021 #335

Day-238 "Cosmos"

I knew a man
Who didn't know time
It didn't seem to matter
He had a great mind
And was very kind

His moments I care not to lose
His life has many a rhyme

2/5/2021 #336

Day-238 "Now"

I spent some time with a man
Who confessed
He couldn't see time
I thought him insane

When he said, isn't it beautiful
I asked, what is it you see?

He smiled and replied

 "Now"

2/5/2021 #337

Day-238 "A Poet's Verse"

Chasing dreams
With never ending themes

Penning devotions
Full of emotions

Defining new ways
Retrying our days

Living to love
Loving to live

Crying with some
Laughing with some

A poet's verse
Is never done

                                                2/5/2021 #338

Day-238 "Rise Up"

Rise up!
Rise up my friend Rise up!
The dawning light
Shines on the western sky
Mountain peaks are dressed in snow
Bluebirds singing sweet hellos
Miracles of life as far as eyes can see
Tis time to catch the day
Don't let it slip away
Rise up!
Rise up my friend Rise up!

                                                  2/5/2021 #339

Day-238 "Questions"

Do you live your days?
    Or
Do your days live you?

Do you know love?
    Or
Does love know you?

Do you live to love?
    Or
Do you love to live?

Do you smile when you're happy?
    Or
Happy that you can smile?

Do you want to do it?
    Or
Do you just do it?

If I don't stop
Writing these lines
I'll never get to "Drink my wine
Or smoke that joint........ Adios Amigo!
                                  2/5/2021 #340

Day-241 "Moments"

Life is but
A sunrise
A love
A laugh
A pain
A word
A moment I want to read
Every single day   2/8/2021 #341

Day-241 "Simple Pleasures"

They're very easy to define
Though some never take the time
They're but butterflies in the mind

Think not that yours are
Much better than mine
For pleasure is what pleasure is
No matter what the time

Reddish sun rising over an eastern plain
Rainbows painted gold
Sunsets from a mountain top
Harvest moon over distant hill
For pleasure is what pleasure is

Sharing a glass of wine
Holding your lover's hand
Pillow talk late at night
Running naked on a shore
For pleasure is what pleasure is

Playing catch with your son
Skipping rocks across a pond
Teatime with your daughter
Swinging in the park
Pleasure is what pleasure is

A hot bath on a winter's eve
Skating on a frozen pond
Reminiscing with a friend
Riding horses in the dawn
Pleasure is what pleasure is

Laughing at silly jokes
A drive without a plan
Playing checkers in the park
Reading beautiful lines
Pleasure is what pleasure is

Never lose your pleasures
As simple as they are
Think not that yours are
Much better than mine
For pleasure is what pleasure is
No matter what the time

                              2/8/2021 #342

Day- 242 "It Is What It Is"

Beauty is what Beauty is
Love is what Love is
Happy is what Happy is
They can tell you lies
Or shape your lives
Yours only to define

                              2/9/2021 #343

Day-243 "Selfies"

They are but moments
Lasting but a second
They're much like life
You wait
You choose
You snap the pose
Is this who we've become?
Marshmallows on a stick?

                              2/10/2021 #344

Day-243 "Little Boys"

From my box
I took a toy.
It was my favorite one.
I gave it to a boy
Who had none
So, he could know
Something fun.

                                        2/10/2021 #345

Day-244 "The Eternal Optimist"

No Matter
The Heat
The Hail
The Snow
The Cold
The Wind
He'll plant it in the ground
And watch it grow.

                                        2/11/2021 #346

Day-244 "Changing Courses"

Changes come like seasons
The greening of the trees
After cold winter nights
Heat and rain after blooming buds
Golden leaves and ripening fields
Harvests due and pending snows
Seasons come and seasons go
Some slow while others fast
No matter if you're young or old
Ages come and ages go
You are but a season
Waiting to change

                                        2/11/2021 # 347

Day-245 "To My Sweet Valentine"

Yes, there were tears
And yes, there were fears
Yet, over the years,
There's been plenty to cheer
For all we've held dear

Sometimes we've whined
Yet often we've rhymed
But a glass of wine
And a valentine kiss
Has never left us a-miss

So on this heart shaped day
I'll give you what may
This poem as a lei
To cherish in your heart
Till life tears us apart

Happy Valentine's Day My Love   2/12/2021 #348

Day-247 "I Am Who I Am"

I am a Man
You can't understand
Unless you know
Who I am.

No matter the color of my skin
You can't understand
Who I am
Unless you know
From where I came
     Or
Why I came.

If you don't know my father,
My grandfather,
My people long gone;
You can't understand
Who I am
Or
Why I am.

But I am a Man;
That, you can understand

You choose to judge;
But you don't understand
Who I am
 Or
Why I am
 Or
From whom I came.

But I am a Man.
That you should understand
 For
Who I am
 Is
Why I am
Who I am.

You should understand
That I am much like you.
For, I am a Man.
That, you can understand.
Caution your judgments please.

Why can't you understand?

2/15/2021 #349

Day-247 "Fifteen Planks"

Fifteen planks upon my back
Fifteen planks to bridge this gap
Fifteen planks we'll soon arrive
Fifteen planks we will survive
Fifteen planks no more despair
Fifteen planks to lay with care
Prepare the bells with joyful sounds
Fifteen planks will bridge this gap.

2/15/2021 #350

My 365 journey is nearing an end. The question I have to ask is, will it ever end?

Day-248 "Winter's Wrath"

From out of the north
The cold winds blew
Hell's inferno turned blistery cold
The Devil himself all
Bundled in ice coated steel;
His snarly, crackling laughter
Piercing the barren air.

His staff, a brazened fork,
Pierced all who ventured out
Searing holes in sockless shoes.
His razor-sharp eyes
Turned pathways glazed
To monstrous graves.

Eternity could not be worse
This inferno from the north.

From out of the south
The warm winds came.
Across the Heavens,
In a chariot of golden sun rays
Pulled by a hundred whited steeds
Apollo took aim.

Over the plains they clashed;
Spears and swords took many a soul
White sheets covered the deadly fields.

The north wind hissed.
The south wind kissed.

Apollo cried out
"My blood runs hot
Forsake me not."

From his scabbard a diamond blade flew
Cutting the breath of that mighty
South bound wind.
He ripped the armor
From the Devil's redden skin
And turned it to dust; then
Took that angry man's staff and threw
It to the sea.

With that the skies began to calm
And the wind turned warm.

Above the plains
In the setting sun
Selene stood proud.
As she glazed the sea
With an orangish glow
A smile on her face
For Apollo her man,
Boreas he tamed.

2/16/2021 #351

On February the 12th 2021 some of the coldest days in over 100 years dove across the Midwest bringing with is blizzard like conditions. From the Canadian border to the Gulf of Mexico it wreaked havoc of all in its deadly path with the most damage done in Texas. This is my rendition of that deadly storm. It also reminds me of the battle between good and evil. How, in the end Good conquers evil.

Day-250 "Worlds Apart"

Lucca, Italy

This red cloth
Was set for two
Yet no one came
When COVID reigned.

A memorial of
Time that was
When we were gay
And shared this space.

A memorial to
Time that will
Again delight
This space we'll seek.

We'll dream and laugh
Tell tales of lover's past.
We'll sip Chianti Supreme
And lunch on delicacies.

We'll toast our lives that
Are yet to be.
We'll bask in the sun
As lover's stroll by.

Once again, I'll
Cross the seas
You, my lover,
I need to please,
At this café,
At a table for two,
As a Tuscany breeze
Blows lavender through your hair.

2/19/2021 #352

Day-253 "Why I Write Joy"

If there is no Joy in the poet
There is no Joy in the reader

I bought some Joy today
To see if it would grow
I gave some to a preacher friend
To see if he could make me whole
He turned and laughed at me
And threw it in a hole
Unbeknownst to him it
Grew and grew and grew.

I dressed in sillies yesterday
Of pinks, and purples and plaids
Thinking someone might see me
With my back against the wall.

Unbeknownst to me
The wall was a blend of
Purple pinks and plaids
And I am color blind

I found Joy the other day
I found it quite gay
It lives in a hole
Inside your soul
You can find it too
Just pen some silly thoughts

If there is no Joy in the poet
There is no Joy in the reader

Why I write Joy?
It's just my Job

2/22/2021 #353

Day-254 "Sail Away"

Sail away, sail away!
Come sail away with me.
Hoist you sails and sail away
To a cosmic land of fairytale dreams
And magical themes,
Where poppycock grows
On mystical trees
And ladybirds sing
In cryptic melodies.
Come sail away, sail away with me

Fly away, fly away!
Come fly away with me.
Flail your wings and fly away
On a summertime breeze to a
Snowcapped Mountain in Belize.
Wherever that may be.
We'll sit on a boulder
And gaze at the sea;
Chase butterflies
As we please.
Come fly away, fly away with me.

Let it be, let it be!
Let it be with me.
It's all hidden up here inside.
I'll lend you a key
If you decide
To let it be.
Come sail away, sail away with me.
My mind an uncharted sea.

2/23/2021 #354

Day-256 "Afternoon Delight"

I'm lying with a woman
Who knows no cloth
A bottle of red wine
And a fire blazing hot.

                                         2/25/2021 #355

Day-256 "Lovers"

Love me in the night

Cherish me in the light

                                         2/25/2020 #356

Day-256 "Snow Flurries"

Softly falling from the sky
Little angels fluttering by
As matrons to a bride
Dressing Mother Earth
Covering her nakedness in
Veils of white cloth
Beautifying her imperfections
Reshaping her sculptured form
There is much beauty
In the falling of the snow
The divine purity of it all
Is solace to the soul.

We dress ourselves in colors
To beautify our inner sides
Much like the falling snow
Outside my windowpane

                                         2/25/2021 #357

Day-257 "Oh to Be A Poem"

What glee
I would be free

What fun
I would embrace the sun

Such beautiful words
I would unravel crosswords

Such magnificent lines
I would forever rhyme

I would soar to the sky
Make love in Shanghai

Climb Mountains in Peru
Drink of the morning Dew

Swing through the trees
On a trapeze

Drink Chablis
On the isle of Capri

Would make my heart shine
I would never decline

Oh, to be a poem
If I could only rhyme

2/26/2021 #358

Day-258 "I Would Love To Be That Poem"

I would love to be a poem
Take you on a journey of the mind
Take you places you have never seen
Touch your heart with many rhymes
Make you laugh when you are sad
Shower you with love when you're in need
So many stanzas yet to script
I would love to be that poem

2/27/2021 #359

Day-261 "I Would Love To Be The Poem"

I would love to be the poem
That brought a smile to your face
That brought comfort to your soul
That brought love to your door
So many poems I would love to be

3/2/2021 #360

Day-261 "I Would Love To Be The Poem #2"

I would love to be the poem
The poem that Lincoln spoke at Gettysburg
The poem that Jesus spoke on the Mount
The poem of King's, "I Have a Dream"
I would love to be the poem
For all the peacekeepers of this world
So many poems I would love to be

3/2/2021 #361

Day-261 "I Would Love To Be The Poem #3"

I would love to be the poem
That ended sadness, grief and crime
That ended hunger, fear and death
That ended anger, hate and deceit
That ended war, race and sexuality
That showed us how to live in harmony
With all men, of all mankind
The poem that ended pain
So many poems I would love to be

3/2/2021 #362

Day-261 "I Would Love To Be The Poem #4"

I would love to be the poem
You wrote when I didn't care
You wrote when I didn't love
You wrote when I didn't see
The love you had for me
The fool I was
I would love to be that poem
So many poems I could have been

3/2/2021 #363

Day-261 "I Would Love To Be The Poem #5"

I would love to be the poem
A mother reads to her newborn
A father speaks to his only son
A daughter recites to her first love
A son pens to his lovely bride
I would love to be that poem
So many poems I would love to be

3/2/2021 #364

Day-261 "I Would Love To Be The Poem #365"

I would love to be the poem
That speaks of sunshine at break of day
That tells of rainbows after rain
That pens sunsets in twilight hours
That traces stars across the heavens
That brings us joy when we are sad
That builds bridges over those "Valleys of Despair"

So many poems I would love to be
I would love to be that poem
That bugles play at the end of day

        3/2/2021 #365

The End of My Journey

This concludes the 365th poem that I set out to write when I began this journey to write 365 poems in 365 days. I completed this task in 261 days. The primary purpose of this journey was to help me overcome the depression associated with the COVID pandemic. The fact that we had to shelter inside our homes for extended periods of time created many a daily challenge for many of us. The fact that we couldn't see our children or our loved ones; that we couldn't eat out or go places or visit with our friends; the fact that we had to endure some police atrocities and marches on our capital; the fact that we had a president that persisted in defying science and spread malicious lies. So many things could have gone, oh so much, much better.

My message to all is that you must have hope and that you have to put on a positive face. Always be the eternal optimist even in the most difficult of times. I guess that is the farmer in me; "Plant it and it will grow". I forever think of those poor people in Leningrad in 1942. Or the Jews slaughtered in the same war; the lost refuges to the Mediterranean Sea or the poor children on our southern border; the many wars in our African States. Dear God, how fortunate we are. We certainly have nothing to complain about. As we don't know hunger, pain or fear on those most horrible of horrible scales.

The task at hand was to write these poems without negative words or thoughts. They were to be happy poems. I found it quite difficult at times and I know that I slipped every once in a while. Yes, I did write other poems, but I really tried not to pollute my mind with negative thoughts. In the end I felt like I accomplished the task even if there was no consistent theme. To have a consistent theme was not my goal. My goal was just to write something as often as I could. Some days were good, and some days were bad; that I admit. They are but reflections of my mind at those particular times. So, sorry folks for I am not a pro and I didn't want to pen verses that were difficult to comprehend. I intended them for the masses, which I hope you understand.

The question remains
Where do I go from here????

LON WARTMAN
Photographer/Poet

Photography and poetry have always been my most favored pastimes, both "capture the moment". I grew up in southwest Kansas where I ranched and farmed for a good portion of my life. During those years I spent untold hours on either a horse or a tractor. Those hours gave me ample time to think and spin tales in my brain. I have also been involved in politics, the arts and numerous civic organizations. I have spent the last twenty years as a commercial appraiser and am now pursuing my lifelong passion of being a photographer/poet. I currently live in Monument, Colorado.

A quiet walk in a forest,
A late night on Times Square,
Stoking a fire as snowflakes fall,
A purple sunset
These are the moments we live
Moments meant to be shared
My gift to you
"Enjoy"

lwartman21@yahoo.com

www.ingramcontent.com/pod-product-compliance
Lightning Source LLC
Chambersburg PA
CBHW041312240426
43669CB00023B/2960